DEATH: THE RIDDLE
AND THE MYSTERY

DEATH: THE RIDDLE AND THE MYSTERY

Eberhard Jüngel

TRANSLATED BY
IAIN AND UTE NICOL

THE WESTMINSTER PRESS
PHILADELPHIA

This book was first published in German by
Kreuz-Verlag Erich Breitsohl und Co. KG,
D-7000 Stuttgart 80, under the title *Tod*
(Themen der Theologie, Band 8).
© 1971 Kreuz-Verlag Stuttgart

PUBLISHED BY THE WESTMINSTER PRESS®
PHILADELPHIA, PENNSYLVANIA

PRINTED IN THE UNITED STATES OF AMERICA

Library of Congress Cataloging in Publication Data

Jüngel, Eberhard.
  Death, the riddle and the mystery.

  Translation of Tod.
  Bibliography: p.
  1. Death. I. Title.
BT825.J8413 1975   236'.1   74-28021
ISBN 0-664-20821-5

To
Siegfried Ringhandt
and
Kurt Scharf
Pastoribus Pastorum

Contents

Preface

We cannot apprehend death in its own terms. Death is mute. And it renders us speechless. If we are to speak about death at all, then a word must come from 'beyond' death. Christian faith makes the claim that it has heard such a word. It has earned the title 'Word of God'. It is with the help of this word that it embarks on its enquiry about death.

This book is an attempt to pose the question of death in such a way that an answer from faith is made possible. There is a great danger that edifying speeches on the subject of death may serve only to explain away the bitter inevitability of our own death and also the pain which we feel at the death of another. Christian faith must resist this danger. Thus only in an indirect sense may this volume be called what used to be termed 'a comforting and edifying book'. It demands thought.

The approach is only to a certain extent academic. However, our intention is not to hinder but to encourage thoughtful participation. In this respect, my Tübingen assistants, Eberhard Lempp and Lukas Spinner have been of great help to me. Robert Leuenberger, my colleague in Zürich, and myself, engaged in an intensive dialogue on the problems which are dealt with in this book over several semesters. This gave rise to a considerable measure of agreement between us. I have much to thank him for. My thanks are also due to Rudolf Smend in Münster/Göttingen for his help and advice in connection with the Old Testament. Even when I felt I must decide otherwise, from among the many theological publications on the subject of death those which impressed and influenced me most were Karl Barth's *Church Dogmatics* III/2 and IV/1, Karl Rahner's *Theology of Death* and Gerd Schunack's study *Das hermeneutische Problem des Todes*. Since the publication of this book we have R. Leuenberger's *Der Tod, Schicksal und Aufgabe*.

The following pages are dedicated to two leaders of the church. In the best sense of the term they may be called 'pastores pastorum'. Theology owes a great debt to them, and for my part at least I would like to express my thanks to them in this way. The fact that both names appear together here will be misunderstood, no doubt for ecclesiastical-political reasons. But it will be misunderstood only by the person who *wants* to misunderstand and who for that reason would seem determined simply to demonstrate his ill-will. But this book is written also for this kind of man. For all men are mortal . . .

EBERHARD JÜNGEL

PART ONE

THE RIDDLE OF DEATH

1. My Own Death
(Death as One of Life's Questions)

What is death?
Most alien yet most our own
Is there anyone we can consult about death?
Putting the question to the living—the anthropological view of death
The dying from the standpoint of medical science—the biological view of death
The validity of a theological solution

2. The Death of the Other Person
(Death as a Social Fact)

Human life in its relation to the death of the other person
Attitudes to death
The theological notion of resurrection in relation to the tendency to assume no attitude to death

3. The Death of Socrates
(Death as the Soul's Release from the Body)

On surrendering a conception
The immortality of the soul—the legacy of Socrates
Death and knowledge—defining the relationship between them
The de-Platonising of Christianity—a theological task

Chapter One

My Own Death
(Death as One of Life's Questions)

What is death?

Life has many facets. The same is true of death. Abraham died in a good old age. Saul took the sword and fell by the sword. His son, Jonathan, David's loyal friend, was slain in the prime of youth. Judas, the betrayer, went and hanged himself. Enoch, however, was taken by God and seen no more. What is death?[1]

Children have been killed by avalanches while playing and laughing together. Unlike soldiers who can be held responsible for shooting women, children and hostages, we cannot say that avalanches are 'responsible'. What is death? How is it that on the one hand we can be held responsible for it, while on the other we see it as completely alien and can respond to it only with speechless and passive helplessness? Is death the natural end to the history of each individual? Or is it a historical disturbance within the well-ordered process of nature?

The neurotic is hindered from being himself. Lacking the capacity to realise himself he suffers a sickness unto death. Pensioners, who because of retirement are deprived of an active relationship to the future face the threat of what has been called 'death by retirement'.[2] Is death already the beginning of the end of the future of one's temporal life? Or can we only properly speak of death in the case where a man's life no longer has any future at all?

Instead of being honoured by the state, Socrates was condemned to death. He refused to accept the chance to escape to

---

[1]See pp. 137–141 for details of all notes and bibliographical references, indicated throughout this book by superior numerals.

freedom and drank the cup of poison as a means toward a higher freedom, a freedom which could only be anticipated in thought. He let Asclepius offer up a cockerel so that death could be understood as a recovery from the sickness of life. By contrast, landing safely after their space-ship had suffered considerable damage, the astronauts of Apollo 13 were welcomed to the safety of the aircraft-carrier with a prayer of thanksgiving. This is an instance which recalls the attitude of the much more unsocratic worshippers of the Old Testament, the attitude expressed in the Psalms where God is thanked for rescuing men from the danger of death. Hailed by a courageous thinker, feared by men no less brave, death on the one hand appears as an end to be welcomed, while on the other it is regarded as a catastrophic conclusion to life which must at all costs be prevented. What really is death?

When Simeon had seen the infant Jesus in the temple he praised God and said: 'Lord, now lettest thou thy servant depart in peace, according to thy word; for mine eyes have seen thy salvation.'[3] 'See Naples and die'—runs the more or less sentimental saying. What is death when in those moments of spiritual exaltation and in those moments when one's experience of this world is at its most intense, it seems to be divested of its terrors? Abraham died an old man and full of years. In Sachsenhausen, My Lai and Biafra, in concentration camps past and present, young people, hungry for life, have died and still die. The patriarch died the death of old age; this is the death which comes when life expires. Yet countless people die because they are robbed of life. What does death at a ripe old age have in common with the death of a murder victim? How is it that death can occur in such contradictory ways?

In the USA it is known that people on the point of death have had their bodies preserved by deep-freezing. Are they dead? Organ transplants and the conservation of vital fluids require that we make a distinction between man's biological and his personal existence, and that we adopt the category of the biological survival of the organism of the no longer existing person.

On the other hand, people in love frequently claim that in the act of love they experience the immediate presence of death. Thus in the midst of life, the fulfilment of personal existence itself would seem to be an anticipation of death.

Life has many facets. Must we not say that death has even more? With God death has at least this much in common: it is enigmatic, indefinable; 'mors definiri nequit'. What makes it indefinable would seem to be the very certainty of its coming. For *all* men are mortal. And this means that no-one has the mastery of death. To define a thing is to gain control over it. And to imagine that we can define death is to presume that we can be its master. But the opposite would appear to be the case. It is not we who are death's masters; death is our master.

As ruling and as dominant, death would therefore seem to be distinguishable from the general process of transience to which everything that has come to be is subject. Death rules over *men,* and as the end of *human* life it is something different from the mere act of passing away. Of course we speak metaphorically of the death of many things which are transient. We talk of the death of a city, for example, or of a culture; we speak also of the death of a flower. These are ways of speaking which clearly give some indication of the close affinity between death and transience. But death is something *human.* Compared with the phenomenon of transience, which seems to be very closely connected with the process of becoming, death is something quite different. It is a uniquely dominant historical power. The literature of every age provides evidence of just how powerful is even the *language* of death. The language of death—threats, alarms, and also enticement and seduction—shares its power to rule. It holds sway not as a 'brutum factum', not as a naked fact. It shapes man's life at its most fundamental level and determines him in the most human of his relationships. The most sublime lyricism of love perhaps demonstrates this more than the most brutal of wars: death has the power to reign. But can it also be defeated? That is the question.

Most alien yet most our own

All men are mortal. I am a man. Therefore I am mortal. If
'to be mortal' at least means 'necessarily subject to death' then
I also, someday, somewhere and somehow must die. This is a
classical example of a particular kind of logical conclusion from
the text books of logic. There, however, the conclusion does
not normally refer to me, but rather to Socrates, Caius, or
A. N. Other. Nor is this fortuitous.

There is the following passage in Leo Tolstoy's novel on the
death of Ivan Ilyich: 'All his life he had recognised the fact that
that famous syllogism seemed to apply perfectly to Caius, but
it was in no sense applicable to himself. Caius, that is the man,
man in general, and to this conclusion there could be no
objection. However, he was certainly not Caius, nor by any
means man in general . . . Caius is mortal, and it is quite in
order that Caius should die, but I, Vanja, Ivan Ilyich, with all
my thoughts and feelings—that is something entirely
different . . .'

Yet however much he may be determined to differentiate
himself from other people with these reflections on death, Ivan
Ilyich is not only himself, nor is he just anyone at all, he is
Everyman. We know quite well that as individuals each one
of us must die. But we do not really believe it. When it becomes
a matter of our own death, the healthy man's faith in himself
suddenly turns out to be astonishingly vigorous. 'Everyone
regards everyone else as mortal—apart from himself' (Young).[4]
And no less pointed is the way in which this fact has been
expressed in psychoanalytical theory: 'No-one really believes in
his own death' (Freud).[5]

Now this fact would be completely misunderstood if we were
simply to regard it as the subjective and arbitrary impression
of the individual. But it is not the wilfulness of the individual
which gives rise to this impression. It is much rather the
expression of a basic existential situation. In the still profoundly
true chorus of Sophocles' *Antigone* which describes man as the
most mysterious of beings, we are reminded that although man

has the power to meet every possible situation, he is nevertheless helpless when confronted by death. Although it is of man's
essential being to find a way and to take that way, when it
comes to death he discovers that there is no way out. He can
find himself in all that is alien to him. It is only in death that
he cannot find himself. Death remains alien to him. This is
what is expressed in the reflections of the dying Ivan Ilyich and
what we must understand is that this is a basic existential
situation. The idea that this is a purely subjective and
arbitrary matter arises because of the fact that death is the event
which brings my own life to an end and so constitutes an
infinite *offence* to me. As the end of my existence death is the
absolute opposite of my life. And it is precisely as this offensive
opposite that death is part of human life. In this sense it is part
of life from the very beginning. In its strangeness, in its
offensive alien character, death is 'no particular event that must
be named among others because it, too, ultimately happens.
It is not only when he comes to die, but always and
essentially that man is without issue in the face of death.
Insofar as man *is*, he stands in the issuelessness of death'
(Heidegger).[6] Man is aware of the fact that there is no way
out of this. Yet because of death's excessively alien character
he cannot, at least for his own part believe it. The statement:
'all men are mortal' is thus valid in this sense. It is valid, but
precisely with regard to myself, myself alone, it has no validity.

But how do we know that *all* men are mortal, that each one
of us moves, hastens or even rushes toward his own death? The
fact that the unexceptionable logical rigour of this conclusion
appears so existentially insignificant may possibly have something to do with the premise from which these conclusions have
been drawn. The assumption that 'all men are mortal' is
possibly not without its problems. In what sense are we to
understand that 'all men are mortal?'

'Mr. N. will die, because the Duke of Wellington and others
died. We have "taken note" of this in the form "all men
are mortal". Are we to take it that death is an induction!'[7] —

Thus Max Scheler, with a touch of sarcasm. And it is certainly true that to use death as a logical example could provoke considerable sarcasm were it not for the quite justifiable suspicion that by introducing death into the text books of logic we thereby ironise our relationship to it in any case. As an example it loses none of its seriousness. But the question is whether we can take it seriously by merely reading about it. But can we speak seriously about death? Is the event of death not in fact something so serious that anything we say about it must make it seem less serious? Is it not a fact that death causes us more embarrassment than anything else in life? How are we to account for that strange smile which we may often detect when we offer our sympathies to those who mourn? Does death somehow call for irony? How are we otherwise to find protection from it? Is it not in fact true that death, because we have to live with it and come to terms with it, and even though we never really can come to terms with it, is the source and spring of all irony? 'Irony is the infinitely delicate play with nothingness, a playing which is not terrified by it but still pokes its head into the air' (Kierkegaard).[8]

However, irony about death always presupposes the knowledge that our death is inevitable. We do not have access to this knowledge by means of induction. It is when we make the attempt to understand our own lives that we seek the answer to the problem of death. We know that our death is inevitable and we have this knowledge in the form of a *question*. It is not a question which is posed to me by someone else. The question, What is death? is one which is always with us. It is part of the givenness of our lives. It is a question which we can try to suppress, but it will always be there. Even in the question itself death is present. Death, in its inevitability affects us in our very innermost being. It compels us to ask Why? What comes afterwards? When? How am I to understand my death?

Our own death in particular. In a strange way death is part of us even in our questioning it. And this reveals a second basic existential situation which immediately confronts us with the paradox that death is not just entirely alien to human existence; for at the same time it is part of *our innermost being*. If many things in life are uncertain, even if everything is uncertain, death at least is certain. 'Incerta omnia, sola mors certa' (Augustine).[9] Everything can be taken from us, even life itself. But no-one can take death from us. It is an inalienable part of us.

This does not mean that death is now most alien, now most intimately a part of us. It is rather that in experiencing it as essentially part of us we know it to be alien to us. As an essential part of us it remains most alien to us. And it is this which makes death so enigmatic. This is why, in his effort to understand his life, man *asks questions* about death. He does not raise the question of death out of mere curiosity. This is what young children do when they ask questions about it. However, their questions are really aimed at something unknown which is called death, and this is because children cannot grasp the fact that death is essentially part of them and have no notion of death's alien character. That which is most intimately a part of us can never be the object of curiosity. Death is too near to us to become the object of curious enquiry. The enigmatic question of death is much more serious. It touches upon the mystery of life.

Is there anyone we can consult about death?
In order to speak seriously and conscientiously about death, we must have knowledge of it. However, it is uncertain whether anyone can ever be said to have any knowledge of death. It is not that anyone is exempt from it. But the person who is about to die does not yet have any knowledge of death. 'Death is not an event in life: we do not live to experience death', said Wittgenstein,[10] a thinker who always sought after clarity. Another thinker who also aimed at clarity sees the matter differently: 'It is of the *essence* of everyone's

experience of life, and of our own, that our lives are directed toward death. Death is part of the form and structure in which alone life is given, our own life as well as that of others. This is as much the case *from within as well as from an external point of view*' (Scheler).[11] Who is right?

The problem may first of all be treated as one of method. Whom could we consult about death so that we could speak about it seriously? Responsible talk about death must deal in *cases*, with examples which make it possible for us to ask questions about death. But this immediately raises some embarrassing difficulties, for no-one who wishes to raise the question of death has 'experienced' death for himself, and no-one who has had to 'experience' death can be questioned. Man may come very close to death, he may even surrender himself to death. But no-one can experience death itself in such a way that he could provide us with information about it. While seriously intended, Epicurus' old joke, like all sophisms seems to hit the nail on the head: 'Death, the most terrifying evil, does not concern us. For as long as we are, death is not there; when it is, we are not.'[12]

Whom then can we consult about death? The *event of death* itself is not something we can question. It is not even something which we can easily determine. The question as to exactly when the dying person becomes a lifeless corpse is one which even presents doctors with a great many difficulties. The question is in fact so difficult that with some resignation it has been suggested that death should rather be defined in legal terms: as 'consequent upon the coroner's declaration that death has taken place' (according to Scheler).[13] The event of death is mute. Nevertheless, some still have the idea that death speaks. And this has given rise to death being represented in the paradoxical form of a dead man, a skeletal figure which appears to go about as the sad remains of a human being, and which can allegedly confront us and address us. However obviously profound, this is a paradox which can hardly mislead us into thinking that death itself can speak.

Death itself is mute, and it renders us speechless. As long as we are alive, we cannot expect death itself to provide the answer to the question of death.

In this respect, *the dead* and death itself are in the same category. No science can take any oath on the testimony of the dead, not even in the search for an answer to the question of death. No science can do this nor should it wish to. If it did then it would no longer be a science, and if it could then we would have no need of any science. It is with a shudder that theology recalls the story of Saul's oath by the dead at Endor (1 Sam. 28). The episode is expressly characterised as an enterprise set up to end God's silence—a silence which was pregnant enough. As possible cases, as examples to be consulted about death, the dead must be excluded. They are dead.

But what about those who are *dying*? Are they not confronted by death in such a way that they may be able to provide a competent answer to the question of death? The person who knows that his death is at hand may possibly be in a position to answer questions concerning his own particular proximity to death. But this does not mean that he can provide us with information about death itself. A dying person may be existentially closer to death (perhaps!) than a person who is still alive, and with some justification it might be wrong for us to say that he was 'dying'. The fact is that he is still alive. As dying, he is still among the living, and there is an immeasurable distance separating him from the living. Nevertheless, temporal proximity to death cannot conceal the fact that the person who is dying is distinguished more sharply from the dead than from the living. Life's end does not come before the process of dying is complete; the two things are identical. It is only with death that one distinction is abolished and the other permanently constituted, for it is death that makes an infinite qualitative distinction between the dying and the dead. In the process of dying we are still alive. Like the infant about to be born, the dying person may be close to death in a special way. But it is for precisely this reason that he has no knowledge of death, and as a case to be consulted he has no more authority than the living who have not yet entered upon the process of dying.

It may well be that those who are dying yet still alive along with *all the living* constitute the authoritative source for information about death. The fact that many of the living frequently have something significant to say about death is no warrant for this. The decisive thing in this regard is not whether some person can provide comforting or wise thoughts simply because he is among the living. The question is much more whether our life itself has something to convey about death. Can life itself provide us with any knowledge of death? We may answer this question with a cautious 'Yes'.

Putting the question to the living—the anthropological view of death

It is a well known fact that some animals have a kind of presentiment about their death. When they 'realise' that their end is imminent 'they lay themselves down and await their end' (Landsberg).[14] Human life differs in that it is basically determined by having a relationship to death. This is not by any means confined to the presentiment which may arise in the moments which precede death. From the time when the child is about nine years old he realises that everyone must die, himself not excepted. The child of course usually learns about the inevitability of death from adults. Up to this time in the child's life death has a role similar to that which it had in man's pre-history and early history. It is seen to be neither final (irreversible) nor inevitable.

For one thing, we discover that as far as the life of mankind and the life of the child are concerned, a premise about immortality is accepted as self-evident. This is not the kind of immortality which has death as its opposite pole. All the 'proofs' of immortality require the assumption that man's mortality must first be 'proved'. However, this 'proof' of man's mortality can hardly be said to succeed in the form of the logical argument that 'from the many individual deaths we can observe, we may derive the rule that all men are mortal' (against Choron).[15] It is much more likely that the experience of the temporal character of our lives simultaneously provides evidence of our mortality. Through our experience of life as temporal we receive the insight that life has certain *limits,* or *deadlines*. This insight is not something which we have to be taught. It is present in the history of mankind as well as in the history of each individual.[16]

It is for this reason that we share the doubts raised in connection with Voltaire's famous contention that 'if a child were to be brought up alone and taken to a lonely island . . . then he would understand death's inevitability as little as a plant or a cat.' The child does not remain a child. It is an experience to know that one has ceased to be a child. The transience of childhood demonstrates to him the fact, that transience is part of his life. He thereby has the capacity to relate himself in a positive way to this experience of negation. The extent to which this capacity is bound up with the capacity for speech is a question which has to be raised although it is not one which we can pursue further here. Nevertheless, it is most probable that language is the dimension of existence which enables us to relate ourselves to the negations which we experience in a positive way, and to work through the pain of negation in such a way that it can be turned to life's advantage.

We can agree then that *human life stands in a relationship with death*. In his important essay on 'Death and Survival' Max Scheler has turned his attention to this point. Knowing of his own death the living person stands in a relationship to death. 'Even if he were the *only* being on earth, man would in some sense know that death will catch up with him. He would know this even if he had never observed the changes which affect other creatures, changes which eventually transform them into dead corpses.' Scheler's somewhat exaggerated formulation is exactly the opposite of Voltaire's. In the following chapter we shall see to what extent this formulation conceals some other important aspects.

For the moment we are looking for some authoritative source of information about death. We have shown that man's life stands in a relationship with death. And now we can certainly say that this relationship constitutes a source of information. Let us now examine Scheler's ideas a little more closely in this connection.

In life, man's relationship to death is such that death is seen as an event apart from which the living person could not possibly understand his life. Man understands himself as a being who has time (and this is also why he can lack time), and as a being who understands that his time is not unlimited. Both of these aspects define our existence which in all its actions remains temporal in character and which at the same time constantly runs up against its temporal limits. Thus the process of time affecting human life ensures that man knows that his time is limited, or at least that he is to some extent familiar with this condition. For the person who exists in time, time is seen to expire. 'For the young man and the boy, the future which is experienced (or which may yet become his experience?) is present as a broad, bright limitless vista, as an immense field which he sees as "possible material for his experience", a future of which wish, longing and fantasy paint a thousand pictures. But with every fragment of life experienced, as lived in its immediate after-effect, there is the feeling that this broad *prospect* of life-to-be-experienced has contracted.' Scheler has analysed this phenomenon as 'the directed tendency of change' in which there occurs 'the steady *consumption* of that which is regarded as the possible material of experience, the consumption of life given as future by life lived and by its aftermath.' And according to Scheler it is this 'experience of directed change which may also be called the *experience of life's directedness toward death*.'[17]

This experience of being directed toward death constitutes a relationship to death and can tell us something about it.

As far as method is concerned, then, do we now have an acceptable answer to the question of death? We have at least discovered this much: that only man's life itself can be considered to be an authoritative source for information about death. We treat of man's life because it stands in a relationship to death and because this relationship also constitutes its experience. It is also true of course that this experience enables us to come to a more precise understanding of human *life*: as a 'being toward death' (Heidegger). On the other hand, however, from the point of view of method, this can be of considerable gain as far as the question of death is concerned. It can be of help in as much as death is something which can only be understood for what it is from within the horizon of man's life. Therefore in this respect, we may regard the opposite of Epicurus' statement as valid: death concerns us. It is only as long as we are there that death is also there; and when we are not yet or no longer there, then neither is death there. Death lives on life.

However, from our discussion so far the principal conclusion to be drawn is that it is possible for us to know *that* death is. *What* death is is something which appears only on the periphery of our knowledge *that* death is and only in a very vague way. (This is because apart from at least a minimal knowledge of what a thing is there can be no knowledge that it is). Nevertheless, the *question* as to what death is can now be seen to be a meaningful question. Life is the source for information about death. That we shall discover some *answers* and not merely find ourselves confronted with new questions is, with regard to method, something which cannot be decided in advance. But there is much to be gained when we recall that when Augustine gave expression to his existential perplexity at the death of a friend, he not only expressed his own concern, he revealed the whole situation concerning natural man's understanding of death when he wrote: 'factus

eram ipse mihi magna quaestio'[18]—the greatest question
became the question of myself.

To speak of death we must understand something about
life. Do we understand enough about life to be able to speak
about death?

*The dying from the standpoint of medical science—the biological
view of death*

Before we proceed with these methodological considerations
(and although this calls for considerable patience), let us make
an excursus into the field of science. One could argue that
if we are to have any conclusive information about death then
this must be a matter for medical science. Let us therefore
sketch in outline what the science of medicine has to say. Is
there any agreement between the findings of medicine and
the points which we have already discussed? How does
medical science understand the phenomena of death and dying?

(*a*) *Death as an end without beginning.* To Alcmaeon of Croton,
a physician who lived about 500 years before Christ, and who
discovered that the nerves and the brain were the central
organs of the human body, is attributed the following
statement: 'Men pass away, because they cannot unite the
beginning with the end.'[19]

This statement presumably refers to the perishing of the
human body. The human body must perish because men
cannot unite beginning and ending. If man could, then at
the end the beginning would once again be present, and this
would mean that human life also would consist in the eternal
return of the same. This does not happen. Unlike the stars,
which follow their course without ceasing and so continually
unite beginning and ending, and unlike the (at least) apparent
identity of 'nature' which each spring unites the new
beginning to the end, the human body must inevitably perish
never to return. In this sense Diogenes was unique, just as
Napoleon was unique and Mary Smith was, is and will be
unique. As far as human beings are concerned beginning and

end are distinct, and it is for this reason that man's life is not whole. Alcmaeon is suggesting that the human body always has its beginning in the past and its end before it, an end upon which no other beginning succeeds. Thus it is finite in the sense that it is subject to transience.

This doctor of pre-Christian times thought of beginning and end as opposites. Like the philosophy of ancient Greece, Greek medicine concerned itself with the balance of opposites, the equalisation of contrary forces. If being is to be and to flourish, then opposites must either balance or be held in balance.

For medicine then, health is preserved by means of a 'balance of forces', by the balance between the opposite forces of wet and dry, cold and warm, bitter and sweet. If one of the forces is more powerful, or becomes 'monarchic', then health is impaired. However, the physician himself cannot be wholly responsible for maintaining this balance of forces. The maintenance of the balance between beginning and end is not something which is entirely under his control. No human being has the capacity to control this. The farther removed man is from the beginning of his life, the nearer he approaches his end. The closer he comes to the end, the more the beginning is seen to vanish. However, if man is to return to it and be able to begin again, the beginning must be present at the end. Man cannot take his beginning with him, nor can he bring it to an end in order to reunite his beginning and end in death. Man lives between his beginning and his end. He is never at the beginning, (for it always lies behind him); and at the end he is no more. Only as living on this side of both beginning and end is man *between* beginning and end. This is why he is given over to the end with no possibility of making a new beginning. He dies.

This interpretation of a statement made by a physician of the ancient world some 2,500 years ago is not intended as some kind of philosophical flourish but rather as an appropriate introduction to what present-day medicine has to say about death. From the biological point of view, the process which takes place in the course of any human life is one which might be described as an orderly balance between becoming and perishing. 'With regard to its organic structure, parts of the body are more or less completely and repeatedly replaced during life. This process usually goes on so unnoticed that it is withdrawn from general observation. Daily, hundreds of thousands of cells perish to be replaced in the same composition and quantity.' If one were to 'meet and recognise an old friend after ten years'—which among friends is something one ought to expect!—then we could be 'sure that he is likely to possess none of the cells' which he had when we parted ten years ago. 'From the organic standpoint, he is a completely new man' (Nissen).[20] This is what has been termed the balanced alternation between life and death, both forces being present within the same organism. And it was with reference to this process that Goethe formulated his basic law of human nature: 'Die and become.' 'If you do not share this principle of dying and becoming then you will be a sad guest in a cheerless world.'

Life consists precisely in this 'dying and becoming.' We could therefore say that within the time-span of any human life the aim of life is continually to link up and unite the beginning with the end. But even here the result is a kind of *wearing out* of the 'substance of which we are composed' (Schaefer). The second law of thermodynamics is also applicable to the human body. And 'viewed physico-chemically', the fact is that 'the living mass . . . cannot under any circumstances retain its original composition in pure form.' The 'preservation of the so-called optical configuration of asymmetrically composed chemical substances' is also one of the 'remarkable features of the structure of life.' However, the impossibility of guaranteeing this preservation for any length of time means that as far as human life is concerned 'our bodies are condemned to die' (Doerr). In taking place as an organic process, the continual linking of beginning and ending gives precedence to the end over the beginning. The so-called proximity of the processes of becoming and perishing within the one organism, of which life as a matter of fact consists, necessarily results in the suspension of the 'balance of forces'. This disturbance is the quite natural process which in turn leads to what Alcmaeon called the 'monarchy' of perishing. The consequence of the process of alternation between beginning, end and beginning, is that quite naturally the whole man is led to an end which has no beginning. Therefore, where no unnatural disturbance of the balance of forces occurs, such as some unnatural reason for death, then the natural result is the death of old age. This is the definitive end. And with this end, man loses 'his capacity to pass life on as well as his own capacity to live on' (Schaefer).[21] If something of his life is to survive as life then he must take care to arrange for this in time. According to Immanuel Kant, this is the reason why we have the institution of marriage. It may be that life itself has a way of expressing its gratitude to those who agree to this institution in so far as the life-expectation of married people is decidedly higher than that of those who are unmarried.

(*b*) *The definitiveness of death and the reversibility of dying.* When it comes to the question of *determining* the *definitive end* of a human life medical science finds itself faced with considerable difficulties. This is because the unmistakable signs of death appear only after the actual occurrence of death. This is related to the fact that man can be 'survived' by certain of his bodily organs. Organic death and the death of the person are not identical. Different organs of the body also have different rates of survival. It is mainly for this reason that medical science has come to the conclusion that dying does not necessarily have to be an irrevocable transition from life to death. Death from 'unnatural' causes, for example because of illness, can be 'stopped'. This is because dying is not a momentary event but rather a process which is more or less extended in time. This means that such a thing as a return to life is possible. By being able to distinguish between different kinds of 'organic death' it has come to be seen that the boundary between life and death in fact fluctuates. The frontier between life and death has thus become blurred. We may now clarify this in connection with the biological notion of the so-called 'entrance gates of death', the 'atria mortis'.

'In the classical medicine of the ancient world there were four atria mortis, vestibules, or better, entrances for death: the brain, the heart, the lungs and the blood' (Doerr). The cessation of the heart or the breathing are now things which under certain circumstances can be set right. Thus a dying person may be saved from the death which already may appear to have occurred. A man is considered dead only when every effort to revive him has failed. In this way, the dying person benefits from the capacity of the different organs to survive for a longer or shorter period of time. Dying occurs as a *process of interrelation* in which the most important parts of the body have their role to play. The attempt to revive a person is basically an interruption in the process of inter-relation. It is a process which begins among the 'atria mortis' whenever the process of dying sets in. Dying is a vicious circle. When the process begins the current which circulates between the breathing, the brain, the heart and the blood is shut off. 'Every weakening in the strength of the heart lowers the blood pressure. In turn, the nourishment of the heart with blood and other vital substances also decreases. And so this circular process continues . . . It is the same with breathing. Breathing will continue only as long as the brain is well supplied with oxygen. Any damage to the breathing, however, also in turn causes damage to the oxygen supply. We can therefore say with some justification that the entrances of death are characterised by the fact that they operate in a vicious circle. Whatever it may be that triggers off the process of dying, it is a process which ends in death only when the process of interrelation as such is permitted to run its full course. This means therefore that every interruption in the vicious circle halts death' (Schaefer). Interruption is possible because the organs whose activity is less complex have the capacity to survive for a longer period of time and die only at the point when it can be confirmed that organic death has taken place. It is therefore of the utmost importance that this negative process of interrelation occurring among the interdependent organs should be interrupted before organic death takes place.

The criterion for the possibility of successful 'recessation' is determined by the brain's capacity for survival. The brain as such cannot be made to re-function once it has ceased to function. It is because of this particular vulnerability that the brain is called the 'first gate of death'. And the reason for this is that 'after an eight-minute interruption of the blood supply the cerebrum is damaged to such an extent that . . . consciousness never returns . . . There have been cases where the brain has finally ceased to function, the heart having also ceased to function for the same period of time, but where heart and breathing have begun to function again normally. In such cases the body still "lives"; it lives a ghostly, unconscious life' (Schaefer), not a life which is conscious of its existence. In such cases we speak about 'individual death' as distinct from 'biological death'. The distinction is necessary in the sense that 'those structures of the brain which enable us to call the individual a person do not re-assume their normal function.' Medical science refers to this condition as 'decerebration' or as the 'apallic syndrome': 'a living human body, but nevertheless not a living human being! This condition may continue for weeks, months, even years, until the point is reached when due to some complication that life is extinguished.'[22] However, as soon as the cerebrum has finally lost its capacity to function, death has already irrevocably occurred. Thus it is the 'short period of time until the organic death of the brain which decides not only the question of the finality of death and whether, loosely speaking, a return to life may be possible, but also the length of time

involved in the process of dying. In this space of time the
boundary between life and death may be said to shift'
(Kuhlendahl).[23] The doctor thus has to face not only the
question of what medicine can do (and in this respect not
only the doctor but society as well)—but because of this
shifting boundary he also has to deal with the problem
concerning how the dying person may best be helped and
how one may prevent a situation which may turn out to be
worse than death for all those who are involved.

(c) *Signs of approaching death and symptoms of death's occurrence.* The
four 'atria mortis' also provide observable evidence of the
process of dying. Failure of the breathing, in the supply of
oxygen, failure in the circulation of the blood or of the muscles
of the heart, and changes in the blood itself all have observable
consequences. Among the observable signs of death are: 'the
odour of decay in the breath; the "facies hippocratica" with
the sharply profiled nose, the half-open mouth, the dropping
of the eyelids; the involuntary release of urine or faeces; cold
sweat, mucus which cannot be coughed up and which is the
cause of rattling noises. The sense of touch begins to disappear.
The movements of the hands become uncoordinated. Frequently, but not always, first the rational then the sensitive,
animal and finally vegetative functions begin to cease . . . most
people who die from illness are not fully conscious. The
restlessness and the moans of the dying person are caused by
certain reflex processes and do not necessarily signify pain.
As far as one may judge from the biological point of view, a
person's death does not necessarily have to involve any
special agony.'

When death *has occurred,* then the breathing, heart and
pulse stop. 'The skin is cyanotic or pale and insensitive. The
cornea becomes opaque. The pupils widen. The muscles
slacken. The setting in of rigor mortis is variable. After
intense muscular effort rigor mortis can suddenly begin. As a
rule, there is usually an interval of three to ten hours before it

sets in'. When rigor mortis ceases after 24–28 hours, there may then be movements.

Unmistakable signs of death having occurred can be established only after a certain period of time has elapsed. The most certain of these is tissue-decay. 'The cells of the already opaque cornea begin to separate. Some hours later certain dependent parts of the body begin to show livid spots. At first these can be pressed in such a way that they disappear. Later they remain permanent. The skin begins to dry up and the lips in particular take on the appearance of parchment. Due to decay which develops in the bowel the skin of the stomach discolours and becomes greenish. Gases which are produced by this decay cause the abdomen to become distended. Whenever there is sufficient air, dampness and warmth, the tissues progressively decompose due to the presence and activity of bacteria and insect larvae. After a period of four to six years only the skeleton remains.' No doubt this must be the most unmistakable sign that death has occurred.

It is much more difficult to enumerate the *early* signs which would indicate that death has occurred. Earlier signs are not wholly unambiguous. 'In 1874 a special prize was offered to the person who could point to some early sign about which there could be no possible doubt. To this day the award has not been conferred . . . The surest signs appear when the electric stimulation of the nerves and muscles ceases, and when the currents which activate the brain (encephalogram) and the heart (electrocardiogram) stop.' The difficulty of indicating any unmistakable early criteria for determining whether death has occurred is bound up with the phenomenon which we have already mentioned, namely, the shifting boundary between life and death. Since death is not a momentary event, the process of dying is such that it makes it difficult to determine at precisely which point the body becomes a corpse. When one of the life-centres ceases to function, and when the process of feedback stops there is yet the additional fact that thousands of cells which still have the capacity to live are inevitably condemned to death.

It is for this reason that different stages of the death and the dying process in which the human body is involved have been distinguished: clinical death, absolute death and physiological death. The criterion for these distinctions is the meaning of that life which is still latently present in the dead or dying person. This means that precautions can therefore be taken when death is only apparent. It is not when clinical death has been established but only when absolute death can be established with complete certainty that the human body can be declared to be a corpse. And it is only 'when so many cells and tissues have become so severely damaged, and when every possibility of recovery is seen to be finally impossible . . . that the body may be buried' (Faller).[24] It was due to the touching and amusing directness of the poetry of Friederike Kempner, the 'Silesian Swan', that on 7 March, 1871 a waiting-period of five days between death and burial was introduced in Prussia. She writes: 'We want no innovations/, stick to the old custom/ and rush us to our graves/ as though we couldn't wait!/ There's always plenty of time and space for dancers—/, O deluded humanity/, when it comes to mortuaries,/ you're all as bad as you are blind.'

(*d*) *The death of the body—the death of the person.* Biological data about death and the process of dying relates only to this process and its conclusion with regard to the life of the body. But what do we mean by this 'only'? Could anything be clearer than death itself? Or has some important aspect been omitted?

Two further aspects suggest that there might be more to it than this. The *first* concerns *the proportional relationship of life to death from the standpoint of temporal duration.* A person may die early or late in life. The efforts of medicine to restore life to a person presupposes that a distinction must be made between an untimely, early death and a natural death due to old age. Both may occur. Now if death due to old age is defined as the natural consequence resulting from the ageing of the body, as life's latest possible end, then a question arises concerning the significance of the fact that unnatural, untimely death is still as a rule the more frequent. Clearly, death does not merely signify the negation of a particular *reality* (namely, the reality of the person who has lived up to that point). For in addition to this it also signifies the loss of attainable *possibilities* (as far as the person who still had a life to live is concerned). Up to now death has not as a rule been regarded as the end of a reality which has exhausted all its possibilities. However, the question which death now poses is that of the *discrepancy* between the reality of a life lived and the possibilities of a life to be lived.

Over and above this question of death as bodily death there is therefore the further question of death's *historical dimension,* that is, the problem of the relationship between the reality and the possibilities of human life. We can now raise a *second* point. Apart from the physical life of the body we can know nothing about man's life. However, within the structure of our physical life we are aware of the activities of the life of the mind and of the spirit which as such are quite different from physical actions and apart from which man cannot be considered to be man. Man can listen and understand, he can respond and keep silence; he has desires and yet can choose to renounce what he desires; in complete possession of all his physical powers he can undergo un-speakable suffering; he can dream and calculate, he can be good or evil or beyond good and evil. Man can believe, love and hope. We should not of course underestimate the fact that in all this, life from the physical aspect also has a role to play. But such things are not sufficiently explained with reference to physical life alone. They have their source elsewhere. And for this notion of 'elsewhere' tradition provides the concept of *soul* or *spirit* and consequently can speak not only of physical actions and processes but of the actions of the spirit. To what extent are these actions affected by death? What is death if man is not merely a body, but who without a body clearly cannot live? And what is man when death means the destruction of his body thereby bringing his physical and spiritual life to a temporal end?

The validity of a theological solution

So far, with the help of certain questions, we have been attempting to illuminate the riddle of death. Death—so alien and yet so much a part of our lives—what is it? To pose questions is one thing, to find answers quite another. Before we can discover a possible solution (again with the help of some further questions), some indication must be given of *what kind* of possible answer this will be in its relation to the particular framework within which our discussion is set.[25]

This is a *theological* enquiry. In this respect the possible answers are to be sought within the sphere of Christian dogmatics. This is an objective discipline. Its basis and subject-matter is faith in God. Even if in a sense which may vary according to the particular type of discipline, answers which are objective and scientific must be valid and binding. The sense in which the findings of the natural sciences are valid is very different from the sense in which the findings of the human sciences are valid. On the other hand, the nature of the validity of the answers which Christian dogmatics may provide is peculiar to this particular discipline. It deals with a kind of validity which can only be based upon *the validity of faith* itself.

This 'only' here does not in any sense imply that we are now dealing as it were with some less valid kind of validity. There is nothing more binding and valid than faith in God. To this extent we can therefore also say that the validity of a possible answer must be directly related to the validity of faith. And as we have noted, this is a validity of a particular kind.

The validity of the statements of the empirical sciences can be tested, for example, with regard to their verifiability. If a check shows that the statement is correct, then it becomes binding for our understanding: it is to be accepted. The sense in which faith is binding and has validity differs in that it is the *conscience* which is bound, that is, the conscience has certainty of that which is faith's concern. However, to be certain in our conscience, even if we have a 'good conscience', is not necessarily always a good thing. It can possibly even be disastrous for other people. For instance, a man may commit crimes from sheer conscientiousness. In cases such as this, the 'good conscience' is the conscience which is bound in the wrong way. Nor can we exclude the possibility that faith, or rather the sense in which faith has sometimes been understood, may bind conscience in the wrong way. A study of church history will show that this can happen. With regard to the question of its validity then, faith requires some criterion which will determine whether its certainty about that which concerns faith is genuine, that is to say, whether it is bound in the right way. There is such a criterion and that is the criterion of *freedom*. This freedom is certainly the freedom of my own conscience. But this is not to be understood as a freedom which is mine and therefore mine alone. For at the same time and above all else it must be a freedom which effectively enables me to listen to the voice of the freedom of others.

As binding and valid then, genuine faith is a certainty which *frees* us from uncertainty as well as from false ties. Faith gives us the certainty of freedom. It binds the conscience by setting it free. And this is because faith's concern is God. There can be no certainty about God unless we are men who have been set free. A possible answer to the question of death, if it is to be the binding and valid answer to faith, must therefore be an answer which has the power to set man free. If the answer to the question of death is not one which has the power to *set us free* (from uncertainty and from false ties), then this will simply mean that *faith* has no valid answer to this question.

Before we discuss the possibility of there being such an answer, we must at least raise the question of the *necessity* of such an answer. Is there any real necessity for faith to provide a valid answer to the question of death?

There is; for two different reasons, the one christological, the other anthropological. There is a sense in which Christian faith as a whole amounts to an answer to the question of death. The church proclaims the *death* of the Lord' in the expectation that the Lord will 'come' (1 Cor. 11: 26). To this proclamation of the death of the Lord there also belongs the cry of victory. Put in the form of a question it is to be seen as an answer: 'O death where is thy victory? O death where is thy sting?' (1 Cor. 15: 55). Paul's preaching as a whole is to be understood as nothing other than the 'word of the cross' (1 Cor. 1: 18). Here, there can be no doubt that the question of death is answered in a quite definitive way. The answer has its own particular character, but it is this answer which will concern us. In any case, the Christian proclamation does not permit theology to let this question answer itself. The essence of Christian faith is determined by the fact that this is a question which has been answered. The necessary task of theology is to give appropriate expression to this answer in contemporary terms.

The other reason why it is necessary to find an answer to the question of death is somewhat different. The question of death may possibly concern a man in such a way that he may even be induced to react in a dangerous way. The person who is left with no valid answer to the question of death will supply himself with substitute answers. Unable of himself to solve the question of death a person may be plunged into grave uncertainty. His uncertainty is his only answer to the problem. In this regard, uncertainty is not necessarily dangerous, but as a response to the question of death it still has to be taken seriously. However, to be uncertain in this respect is one thing; to have no conscience about it is quite another, and this constitutes a much greater danger. There can be talk of death of a certain kind, and a certain kind of silence about death which betrays a lack of conscience. And if it is possible, it is this which makes it absolutely necessary that a responsible, conscientious answer to the question of death be found. For example, in an attempt to 'come to terms' with it, death may be regarded as a mere bagatelle. But the person who claims to have come to terms with it is a person who is certainly to be mistrusted. Above all, such a person should be suspicious of himself. One may also magnify the importance of death to such an extent that life is made to appear quite trivial. Death thus becomes more worthy of our attention than life, and life is lived only in such a way that death may be allowed to exert its own fascination. We can be fascinated by death. How true this is! We can succumb to its spell. But it is most important to remember that a lack of conscience is something which can easily be exploited. 'Life is not the highest of goods' then becomes the seductive slogan which finds easy acceptance. Logically intolerable and stupid, this is a notion which can be used to mislead us into believing that the allegedly higher goods are not themselves on the side of life. Yet people have chosen to adopt views like this. Their consequences have and always will constitute a permanent danger. Talk of death which betrays a lack of conscience is perilous to life. If it is possible, a valid answer to the question of death is necessary if this is to be prevented.

Chapter Two

The Death of the Other Person
(Death as a Social Fact)

Human life in its relation to the death of the other person
We all have an awareness of our own death. This realisation
has helped to deepen our enquiry. In the preceding section we
discussed the possibility of finding an answer to the question
of death. In this chapter we shall take a further step which
will enable us to move beyond the question in the direction of a
theological answer. This will, at the same time, lead us into even
greater difficulties, as we shall see. But we have no choice but to
face these difficulties with patience. This is the attitude which
every discipline demands and theology is no exception.

We have seen that death is one of the basic factors which
determine our lives. However, of equal importance is the fact
that my life, in all its individuality, is also *socially* determined.
Man is man with others. 'Man is man . . . only among men'
(Fichte).[1] Man conceived of as the 'solitary creature on earth'
would not be a man. It is this which has to be emphasised
against the thesis put forward by Scheler.

If it is correct, Scheler's view that human life is fundamentally
determined by its 'directedness toward death' must also be true
with regard to the fact that human existence is always a being
with others. However true it may be that the individual's life
can be individual only on condition of the possibility of social
life—regardless of whether he manages to achieve this
existentially or not—it is equally true that the relation in
which a man stands to his own death is never merely a
private relationship. If a man's life is always determined by the
relation in which it stands to death, then the other person is
also to be understood as always having a relationship to my

death, and correspondingly, my life also will always be bound up with the death of the other. From the human point of view then, death is just as much a social fact as life itself. 'Vita communis' thus corresponds to 'mors publica'.

The ancient abuse of putting widows to death conveys something of this. So also does the civil law against suicide—a law which is difficult to understand in that against his will the suicide is legally punished by those who are still alive. Paul Landsberg has examined this phenomenon more closely: 'with the death of the other my relationship to him is shattered; but to a certain extent this relationship was constituted by *myself*, and it is precisely to this extent that death penetrates to my innermost existence.'[2]

Thus the phenomenon which Scheler describes with the help of the notion of the 'experience of life's directedness toward death' in no sense applies solely to the relationship in which I stand to my own death. The notion of the 'experience of directedness toward death' must also be further extended to include the life and death of others, and this is primarily because of the temporal structure of that experience. As temporally structured the death-directedness of my life is of significance also for the life of the other person, just as the death-directedness of the life of the other can also determine my life. This is not merely something which has to be considered in connection with the question of leaving an inheritance. The fact is rather that there is a limit to the time which the other can have for me—most of all in fact when he wants to have un-limited time for me. On the other hand, the reverse applies as well, for as my time is more and more taken away from me, it is also taken away from other people. The time which I no longer have for myself is time which I no longer have for others. In life therefore, we are bound up with one another. But at a deeper level it is really this negation which determines our common involvement with one another. It is not that we first have experience of the death of the other; it is rather that we first have experience of the other's directedness toward death as something affecting our own life. The event of death as it actually occurs and touches our life may be the occasion when this will find concrete existential expression. But that which becomes an earnest reality in the actual moment of death is present in every moment of life as the experience of a moment which is always before us. The death of the other, especially that of the neighbour, is a loss which affects my own life. It involves the loss of certain possibilities for my own life. The threat of this loss of possibilities due to the death of the other is one of the factors which determines human life. This enables us to grasp the fact that our life is essentially temporal and historical. The question of the threat posed to me by my own death is something which we have already discovered in connection with our evaluation of biological factors.

Attitudes to death

Our basic contention is that human life is always life in community. This implies that the relationship in which human life stands to death also has a social dimension. However, to judge from the results of *sociological* research, this implication would seem to be mistaken. If the point we are seeking to make is that man's relation to death at the same time always involves a relation to the death of the other, from the standpoint of sociology it is argued that the assumption of an attitude to death is now something relatively rare because the death of the other is an event which has almost ceased to be part of our experience.

The reason given for this is that, for some time, attitudes to death in the western world have been changing in a quite profound way. The fundamental tendency is for death as such to disappear from society. It becomes culturally and socially invisible. The awareness of death is something which is as it were delegated to certain institutions (such as hospitals, old peoples' homes and undertakers). This means that a socially mediated consciousness of death is virtually extinguished.

Contact with death has become indirect. Direct contact with it is limited to only very few groups.

This is a problem which has been investigated by Alois Hahn and the conclusion he comes to is that the simpler the structure of the society the more direct and less indirect is its contact with death. With complex societies it is the opposite; the more complex the society, contact with death is more indirect and less direct. In a society such as our own, which is steadily becoming more and more complex 'we receive reports every day from the newspaper, radio, magazines etc., about the death of all sorts and conditions of people all over the world, known and unknown, though we never see the bodies. By contrast, the individual in primitive societies experiences fewer deaths. However, his knowledge of death is something directly acquired and usually involves direct contact with the body.'[3]

For any member of contemporary society, there has been not only a quantitative but also a qualitative change with regard to the question of contact with death. What does this imply?

It implies that the death of another now means less to me. The reason for this is that in our complex society, the other person fulfils a role on my behalf and in this role he can be quickly replaced. This is similar to the situation where a job vacancy is filled; the new person takes up the position. For me, the other person is no longer irreplaceable.

But to the extent that he is irreplaceable, his death will touch me all the more profoundly. However, in our society, the people with whom I do have such a close relationship are usually to be found within my own age group. That is to say, death will really become part of my experience only when those of my own age group reach the stage where death is no longer far ahead of them. Or, it may become part of my experience because of the rare and infrequent accident. The aged, who formerly were bound up with society, and related to it in a very different way, now live mainly in isolation. And generally, the experience of death is also an isolated experience. Further questions could be raised about this, concerning, for example, the extent to

which the current 'business with death' is necessarily artificial;
the extent to which this might result in our idea of death
becoming brutalised, and whether in turn this might also lead
to the adoption of quite brutal attitudes toward death.

The fact that death is generally something of which our
society only has an indirect awareness is one of the consequences
of the emergence of the bourgeois society with its pathos for
rationality and autonomy and their capacity ·to grasp and
control everything. Death was the only painful irritant which
could disturb it at its roots. The bourgeois self-understanding,
so dependent upon enlightening and enlightened security, could
be threatened only by death. It is with reference to the
bourgeois society of France that Bernhard Groethuysen has
pointed out that 'at the approach of death the citizen seems to
lose all assurance . . . he cannot look death in the face. The
educated layman would prefer not to speak about it at all.'[4]
But a death about which we are silent consumes our capacity
to enjoy life. The result is that one can also die, as Max
Weber put it, not so much satisfied with life, but tired of it.

This is a process which has become more and more intensive,
and to a large extent it is this which determines our
attitude to death. To quote some statements from a few recent
works on the subject: 'Our grandfathers drew up their last will
and testament as a matter of course. The entire family
gathered round the death-bed. The funeral was an event.
Contemporary society has banned death from public life'
(Faller).[5] It is in fact 'one of the assumptions of our culture
to regard death as an unhappy accident, as due to a flaw in the
art of medical technique, the very means which are employed
to prevent it' (v. Ferber).[6] 'The overt technique of the
prevention of death corresponds to the privatisation of death.'
Bound up with this there is also the tendency to eliminate
death from public consciousness. This can also happen at the
scene of a state funeral where mourning becomes—a quite
respectable—piece of theatre—or merely a theatrical spectacle!
'The mourner no longer has any status' (Bally).[7] With those

who have utopian visions of the future, death is also planned away. 'It is most remarkable how little consideration is given in current utopias of the future to death and to the death of history. Death is pushed aside. They refer to a kind of super welfare society with little work, a great deal of automation, the elimination of illness, long life, complete equality of the sexes, the differences between them having been almost evened out, a society in which all internal and external conflicts are eliminated' (Rahner).[8] As a case of first order conflict death cannot be. What one's project is for tomorrow, is something which one clearly wants today.

All sorts of attempts are made to assimilate death to life. But death accommodated to life is not death at all. The more death is regarded as something to be 'treated' the less one can cope with it. Death becomes dressed up and painted over. It is no longer something beautiful only in Hollywood.[9] In Europe we also have our death cosmetics; it is only that they are somewhat more tasteful. In brief: with regard to man's attitudes to death, the tendency is for him more and more to adopt *no attitude* to it at all. It is set aside.

It would be imprecise if this were to be described as the *suppression* of death. This is a description which has been applied at least since the time of Max Scheler and it is one which is still quite frequently put forward today. For good reasons a powerful protest has recently been raised against this 'conservative', cultural-critical view, betraying as it does a pessimistic attitude toward culture.

Alois Hahn has also pointed out that this thesis does not stand up to the test: 'The moment when death is felt to be an immediately imminent threat and so becomes the significant moment with regard to the question of life's "relevance"; it also becomes material for discussion, and efforts are made to discover its possible meanings.' In old peoples' homes death is something which people think about and discuss. The fact that those of other age groups are largely silent about death is because it has not yet become part of their experience. This cannot be said to amount to the 'suppression' of death. It is rather because of a 'fundamental change in the temporal structure of life' that death, 'as a valid aspect of our identity', seems to disappear.

The protest against the view that death is something we suppress has been reinforced by Werner Fuchs. His central concept of natural death is one which we shall have occasion to discuss in our final chapter. What Fuchs has ascertained with regard to the current 'flexibility and variability of man's views of death'[10] is indicative of the fact that a new *attitude to death* (one not yet formed) will yet be found. To this extent the protest against the view that death is something we suppress in no way affects our own thesis that as far as man's attitude toward death is concerned, the tendency is rather to adopt no attitude to it at all.

The theological notion of resurrection in relation to the tendency to assume no attitude to death
When theology gives a valid answer to the question of death the answer will be closely related to conclusions which have already been reached in this particular area of discussion. What form would a theological answer usually take?

Resurrection of the dead: this is the answer which suggests itself as most obvious to the Christian. As it is frequently claimed, Christian faith lives from the hope of the resurrection of the dead. However, the longer we hope the more real is the threat that resurrection will be judged to be an illusion. Living in the present, our lives are determined much more by our past than by some possible future. In a world alienated from Christian faith, the dead—despite our progress in knowledge and ability—are mightier than the living. This, for example, is why the discoveries of scientists now dead continue to influence the decisions of contemporary politicians. The point was already made by Auguste Comte that 'the course of world history is always determined and directed more by the dead and less by the living.'[11] That our relationship to the future is already determined and limited by the burden of the past may also have contributed to the fact that a general 'faith' in eternal life, understood in the sense in which it always has been understood, is out of step with the times.

Is it true to say that Christian faith, with its hope of the resurrection of the dead, is also threatened by the disappearance of this general presupposition, even to the extent that it also will die the death of old age? From the evidence of public opinion polls we are informed that over 40 per cent of the adult population of the Federal Republic of Germany 'believe' in a life after death.[12] What about the German Democratic Republic? But this 'belief' is no longer sufficiently powerful to shape the structures of life in the world. This is what distinguishes it most profoundly, for example, from the faith of the Middle Ages. The *powerlessness* of this 'belief' which many still share (a powerlessness which can also be verified in other respects), is also reflected in the equally significant fact that a considerable number of our contemporaries altogether reject the idea of a life after death, to say nothing of the notion of a resurrection of the dead.

Now it is precisely this change in man's *attitude* toward death (discussed in the previous section) which accounts for the impotence of any *conception* of a resurrection. 'To this extent, modern man no longer believes in an after-life nor that death will be overcome in an after-life. And this is because he has no clear conception of the death which awaits him . . . and whenever there is no direct perception of death . . . *then the consequence must be that the idea of victory over death in an after-life will also fade*' (Scheler).[13] As the conception fades the attitude disappears. This is how changing conceptions of life and death reflect changes in man's attitudes to life and death. In the absence of an attitude the conception becomes inadequate, until the stage is reached when this absence of the attitude renders the conception inconceivable and impossible to understand.

This is something which the Christian proclamation must

take seriously. Faith cannot and does not involve the *demand* that we adopt certain attitudes and conceptions. Its intention is rather to *make them possible*. What is at stake here is the freedom and validity of faith. If it were the case that we could or should demand say, faith in the resurrection, for instance on the authority of the teaching office of the church, then the kind of hermeneutical reflection on theology such as we are engaged in here would become superfluous. We would not be required to reflect upon the conditions which make understanding possible. But, thank God, it is not like this. If we are not to demand faith but to *make it possible*, then we must face up to the current problems which threaten to render it impossible. The problems will not be solved by making empty appeals to the Holy Spirit. For come what may, the Christian proclamation must account for the *kind* of miracles the Holy Spirit must work if Christian talk of God is to address itself to unbelief (and not only to unbelief). In this regard we must give serious thought to the fact that the Holy Spirit works miracles not in spite of but on behalf of the Christian proclamation, and we must also remember that the proclamation itself should be aimed at the actual contemporary situation. This is not to suggest that it should permit itself to come under the spell of the present, nor that it should simply be accommodated to the texture of the contemporary scene. It should much rather *work* at the actual situation of the times and thereby at the spirit of that which is already shaping our future. The most successful remedy in this connection is not only 'ora!', but '*ora et labora!*'.

In accepting this task we must also reconsider whether the usual answer which Christian faith gives to the mystery of death is correct. Does Christian faith really live from the hope in a resurrection of the dead? If we are to be more precise, then what we certainly can say is that Christian faith lives from the *resurrection of Jesus Christ*.

What does this distinction imply? It implies, first of all, that there is a subtle distinction to be made between the one and the many. The subtlety of this distinction also includes the distinction which exists between God and man. Apart from this distinction there would be no Christian faith. By the resurrection of Jesus from the dead he is defined, according to the ancient formula, as the Son of God, who as such, Paul immediately interprets, is the Lord of all men (Rom. 1: 3f.). Even in view of the resurrection which awaits all men, this is something which cannot be said of any other man. Thus it is faith in Jesus Christ the Son of God who has been raised from the dead that is the basis which justifies and empowers the hope in the resurrection of all men (whether they themselves share the same hope or not). This means that Christian faith does not live from the hope of the resurrection of the dead. It is rather that hope in the resurrection lives from faith in Jesus Christ, from faith in the one Jesus of Nazareth who by his resurrection from the dead is made Son of God and Lord. The distinction is therefore not merely to be noted for its subtlety. It is quite decisive.

This, however, does not make the hermeneutical problems any easier. Quite the opposite in fact! For the widespread suspicion with which the notion of resurrection is treated nowadays makes talk of the resurrection of Jesus all the more problematic. This is a factor of considerable importance. If the notion of resurrection were something generally intelligible to people today then few would be likely to take offence at the resurrection of Jesus, even if such an event were to be considered somewhat premature. But that which constitutes the offence is the idea that this resurrection of *the one* should be the ground and basis for the *general* phenomenon of the resurrection. And because of the fact that the notion of resurrection in general is regarded as dubious, faith in the resurrection of Jesus is something about which many people are decidedly sceptical. As David Friedrich Strauss put it: 'Seldom has there been an incredible fact so poorly supported; never one so poorly supported so incredible in itself.'[14]

We are thus confronted with a circle. While faith in the resurrection of Jesus is that which promises the certainty of our own resurrection, the questionableness of the general notion of a future resurrection of all who have died makes faith in the resurrection of Jesus problematic. That upon which our certainty is based would thus seem to be something about which we can be least certain.

Nevertheless, statistics do not decide the truth of a matter. Sociological research into the belief in immortality can give 'neither positive nor negative proof of the (theological) truth of the belief in immortality' (Hahn).[15] And the truth of the event of the resurrection of Jesus remains quite untouched by the results of opinion polls on what Germans 'believe'. Nevertheless, the relationship between this event and our own lives is not unaffected by the spirit of the times. If we want to understand this event which is independent of us (for it is of benefit to us only to the extent that it is understood), then we cannot afford to ignore the changing spirit of the times. Therefore, if the notion of resurrection from the dead is in danger of becoming an anachronism, or if in fact it has become such already, then one of the tasks of theology is to bring Jesus' resurrection anew to expression in such a way that it can create the adoption of a new attitude of human existence to life and death. If the proclamation of the resurrection of Jesus Christ is to be to faith's benefit then theology must gain an understanding of death which will make the adoption of an *attitude* to death possible once again. Such an understanding is to be gained only by reflection upon the death of Jesus Christ.

The consequence of this is that it is only when the death of Christ as an event encountering our lives becomes intelligible in such a way as to render possible to us a new attitude to death, that faith in the resurrection of Jesus as hope in the resurrection of us all can receive a new dynamic. Theologically speaking, everything will depend upon our arriving at a new attitude to the fact of death in our encounter with the death of Jesus Christ.

Chapter Three

The Death of Socrates

(Death as the Soul's Release from the Body)

On surrendering a conception

Not only is Christian faith threatened by the lack of any specific attitude toward death, it is also threatened by alien conceptions which have found a place within the Christian understanding of death. In this chapter we shall describe one of these conceptions as carefully as possible, if only in order to reject it. This will help us to clear the way and create room for a biblical understanding of death.

Doctors of medicine have reminded us that it belongs to the conditions of bodily existence that at any time man can, and that at some time man must cease to exist in the body. Because and to the extent that man has a body, he dies; or better, man dies because and to the extent that he is body. From this premiss there follow certain differing and even contradictory consequences.

(*a*) When a man dies, because and to the extent that he is body, then one consequence which suggests itself is that man does not really die at all. Why? Because at the same time man is *something other than body*. Thus because and to the extent that he is *soul or spirit* he does not die. Man's mortal body is thus to be seen as contrasted with his immortal soul (or spirit).

(*b*) When a man dies because and to the extent that he is body, then the opposite conclusion which may be drawn is that in body and as body the *whole man* is subject to death.

The first position, the view that the human soul has no temporal end, that it is immortal or indestructible, was one which formed part of the teaching of the ancient and mediaeval church. It is a view which has also been widely taught in modern theology. It is only since relatively recent times that protestant-evangelical theologians have raised objections to this doctrine. Their objections could not be raised merely against the doctrine of the immortality or imperishability of the soul and the understanding of death with which this doctrine was bound up. They found themselves compelled to object to the whole anthropology upon which this conception of death was based. This was discovered to be all the more difficult because the anthropological basis for the doctrine of the immortality of the soul had long been associated with biblical modes of speech. The language of the Bible had even become a weapon in the hands of those who opposed a theological anthropology. Thus in the struggle to arrive at a proper understanding of death, theological anthropology had first to win back its own weapons. The opponent in the struggle took the form of a particular tradition, one which with good justification has been described as the most influential tradition in European thought. We are referring of course to Plato and the consequences of his teaching.

The immortality of the soul—the legacy of Socrates

In his 'Protrepticus' (an exhortation to philosophise), the young Aristotle compares the human soul in its relation to the body to the fate of some men who had been taken prisoner by Etruscan pirates. These Etruscan pirates were particularly unpleasant, as we may judge from the way in which they treated their prisoners. In order to torture their prisoners 'the pirates bound each one face to face with a corpse. In this violent conjunction of life with decay they let their prisoners slowly starve to death.'[1] According to Aristotle, the soul in its body is like the prisoner of an Etruscan pirate bound to a corpse. According to this macabre parable, man's life can be summed up as an involuntary bondage to that which is subject to decay. This means that death, man's real death, can be understood as the soul's *freedom* from its bondage to a decaying body. 'Life makes for the death of the soul; death is the breakthrough to a higher life' (Jaeger).[2] In the violent colours

of this parable the young Aristotle puts forward a theory which
he had learned in the school of his great teacher Plato.
Plato himself had frequently given expression to his views on
the matter. His views on death are based upon the anthropological presupposition that man is the being who is destined for
knowledge. According to Plato, knowledge is not something
which belongs to man. It is rather that man belongs to
knowledge. In the strict sense, however, there is no such thing
as a Platonic anthropology. We can only say that his
anthropology is really an aspect of his ontology. Man's true
essence is deduced from what is understood to be the essence
of knowledge. From what is the essence of knowledge, certain
conclusions can be drawn concerning man's death, which,
whatever else it may be, is something quite different from
man's end.

Platonic views on death have always had an unrivalled
influence. Even today it is difficult to escape their impact.
Any theology or philosophy which has not felt the temptations
of Platonism has no real understanding of itself and is hardly
worthy of the name. This is also true, and possibly most true,
of Plato's views on death. We are impressed by the un-
paralleled unity and strict development of his thought; by the
immense enjoyment which he takes at making words fight and
play gracefully with one another; and by his metaphysical and
political concern for truth. Yet there is something even more
important. For as a whole, his thought mediates an existential
experience which was initiated by the death of another person,
an experience which despite the lapse of thousands of years
still speaks to us and moves us. To an extent which we can
hardly estimate, and in a way which we cannot fully grasp,
Plato's thought was inspired by the death of Socrates.

Among the Platonic texts which refer to the death of
Socrates, those which are historically most important are the
ones which deal with his execution, the texts which are taken to
be the speeches of the teacher himself. They are to be found
in the Dialogue 'Phaedo', so named after one of Socrates

well-loved young pupils. Nor is it accidental that Plato should
have named this Dialogue after the young student; for, as he
suggests, love and death constitute a contradictory yet unitary
tension (according to Paul Friedländer).[3] In the 'Phaedo',
death is described as 'the release and separation of the soul
from the body' (64C).[4] We know that this definition is
derived from the Platonic Socrates. It is regarded as a correct
and self-evident presupposition. In Christianity also it has been
regarded as a self-evident assumption even to the extent that
it has been argued that 'from the theological point of view,
it is to be regarded as the classical description of death'
(K. Rahner).[5] This understanding of death as the release of the
soul from the body can be interpreted in different ways. For
example, in the 'Phaedo' Socrates had to take account of the
view that the soul, once it was separated from the body,
would perish, as it were, 'be dissipated like breath or smoke'
(70A),[6] more quickly than the body from which it had been
released. Descriptions of death such as this prompt the
Platonic Socrates to interpret this understanding of death as
the separation of the soul from the body in terms of the soul's
immortality or indestructibility. There is a whole chain of
'proofs' for this in the 'Phaedo'. The aim of these proofs is to
interpret the release of the soul from the body as a 'refining'
of the soul, as an event which the philosopher may joyfully
anticipate. The presupposition upon which this interpretation
is based is the view that the body is the soul's polar opposite.
However, in order to be, the body is dependent upon the soul
as its life-principle. But at the same time, the body continually
proves to be a hindrance to the soul in its essential quest.
For the soul's true end is knowledge, the vision of that which is
truly real. When knowledge grasps the soul it is released from
transient appearances. It lays hold of 'the things themselves',
those things which never pass away. Nevertheless, when it
seeks to direct itself entirely away from the things which
appear, the soul is continually frustrated by the body. The
senses mediate a kind of 'knowledge' which is essentially

misleading and so prevent the attainment of true knowledge. But since the body perishes because it attaches itself to that which is perishable, the soul is immortal because it attends to that which is imperishable and indestructible. Thus 'when death comes to a man, the mortal part of him dies, but the immortal part retires at the approach of death and escapes unharmed and indestructible' (106E).[7] Now unhindered, the soul may at last fulfil its proper function which is to know the truth.

At the beginning of the 'Phaedo' Socrates is warned by the guard who is to administer the poison that he should talk as little as possible, otherwise the poison will not do its work quickly enough and will have to be administered a second or even a third time. To this Socrates replies that they should go ahead and prepare the poison 'for administering it twice or three times if necessary' (63E).[8] What is of importance to him is only, as he says later, that the argument ('Logos'), the way to truth, should not be allowed to die (89B).[9] The scene is highly significant. For one thing, the phrase 'even twice or three times' recalls a saying which is also quoted by Plato which runs: 'even twice or three times—*the good*.' To request the death dealing poison even twice or three times means that death is awaited as a blessing. The last wish of the dying Socrates is also that Asclepius should offer up a cockerel—the custom which is followed when one recovers from an illness. Thus for the man whose true end is knowledge, death is a *release*. Death, as the release and separation of the soul from the body means that the soul is set free for itself and to be itself.

Death as the celebration of freedom—for Plato also there is something intoxicating about this idea. Yet he overcomes the inclination to bring about this celebration of freedom because he bears responsibility for the 'Logos' which should not die and for which man must care to the last moment of his life. According to a myth recounted by Socrates, the soul's future freedom is measured by the extent to which it has endeavoured to attain to knowledge in life (113D).[10] The blessing of death is something which no man can gain by force. Men must be on guard. The duty of watchfulness is one from which they are never relieved. To witness death as life's fulfilment with one's own eyes does not mean that a consummation is achieved. It is rather that care and attention for the 'Logos' attracts man's interest away from death 'to life . . . to the life which looks this death in the face' (Friedländer)—as in the parable of the cave. To the fullest possible extent, life must serve knowledge unto death. Pure knowledge can be attained only by the soul which has been released from the body. But life is the training ground for the attainment of this state. Therefore although the philosopher can attain his beloved 'Sophia' only in death, he may nevertheless live a life dedicated to the love of wisdom by attempting as far as possible to keep his soul pure from the body—until the God himself sets him free. That which death effects, the release of the soul from the body, becomes the model for the life of the philosopher.

As Cicero was later to interpret this idea: 'Tota enim philosophorum commentatio mortis est'—'for the entire life of the philosopher is marked by the thought of death.'[11] However, this 'commentatio mortis' is not a passive meditation, (we may recall here the provocative disputations of Socrates which finally led to his death). It rather describes the soul in its active struggle for knowledge. Death, as the release and separation of the soul from the body, demonstrates what true knowledge is, for once set free from the body the soul is permitted to come to itself. 'Memento mori' means 'gnothi sauton'. 'Remember that you will die'—the strange counsel with which the Trappists were later to greet each other, merges with the ancient Delphic warning: 'know yourself'.

Death and knowledge—defining the relationship between them
'Memento mori' means 'gnothi sauton'. In the National Museum in Rome there is an ancient mosaic which gives

emphatic expression to the classical philosophical understanding of death. It depicts the form of a man, not a skeleton and yet more in the form of a skeleton than anything else. It may be that it still has skin and muscles, for the attitude of the body—as it lies rather than sits—still expresses movement and life. Yet these traces of the body's movement which can still be discerned seem to move away from the body. The life and movement still present in this human figure express the end to which it has come, that its life has been extinguished. They are an indication of lifelessness and rigor mortis. The hint of flesh and muscles serve only to point to the skeleton beneath which in the end is all that remains. It is this which is the controlling and most prominent aspect of this picture of a still living human being. Lying rather than seated, disembodied yet still in the flesh, moving yet almost lifeless— that is man. In this mosaic all the movement is directed away from flesh and blood and from bodily life. Everything points away toward death. The words beneath this picture could well be 'memento mori'.

Yet beneath this human figure pictured in the form of death there stands in large Greek letters GNOTHI SAUTON! These words are neither the signature nor the 'title' of the 'picture'. Occupying almost a third of the surface of the mosaic they are part of the mosaic itself. The one thing which indicates that the man depicted here is still alive and which constitutes the climax of the movement which still runs through the figure is the large index finger. With this finger, anatomically ill-proportioned yet aesthetically extremely well-proportioned, this man in whom death has so visibly taken shape points to these two words: GNOTHI SAUTON, know yourself.

The mosaic has a great deal to say. It addresses us directly. It has something to communicate. Death, as it confronts us here, clearly compels the observer to seek self-knowledge. The living are summoned to seek self-knowledge not simply because they are still alive but because they will cease to live. It is

important to note that the observer is also included in the
mosaic. Facing this image he is confronted with his death,
and in being confronted with his death it is intended that he
should in turn be confronted with himself: know yourself. In
this sense 'memento mori' can mean 'gnothi sauton'. Remember
that you will die, *therefore* know yourself. Faced with the
inevitable loss of their lives, the living should be moved to find
themselves. But what is it that one discovers in the process of
finding oneself, in the course of one's quest for self-knowledge?
When we pose this question to ourselves then the Delphic
warning will be found to be unsatisfactory. It has to be taken
even further in an attempt to discover the direction in which
human self-knowledge seeks to guide us. In this way the
mosaic can be 'read' in the opposite direction. It can be
interpreted from below to above. Present within and at the
same time confronted by this image we find ourselves involved
in a kind of circle. For the man who seeks self-knowledge knows
this much; he knows that he must die. If he does come to a
genuine discovery of himself through self-knowledge his attention
is thereby drawn away from himself to the fact that there will
be a time when he will live no longer. For whatever it is that
the person with self-knowledge knows about his life is immediately called in question by the fact that in knowing
himself, he knows that he must die. As active in the quest for
self-knowledge, and in the very act of knowing itself, the
human mind recognises, if not in fact at least in thought,
that life issues in death. But what does this 'at least' really
imply!

The significance of this twofold movement which with the
help of the mosaic the observer is able to perceive, can
only be properly evaluated when we recall that man, according
to this particular tradition of the spirit, (the tradition to
which the mosaic also belongs), was defined as the rational
animal, as the 'animal rationale'. Man is distinguished from all
other earthly creatures by his reason; he thus has the capacity to
know and understand himself and also that which is not

himself. At the same time man is also the earthly creature who stands in a relationship to his own death. What is the relationship between *spirit and death*? The usual answer to this question is that it is man's capacity for knowledge that is the basis for the relationship in which he stands to his death. Since man is a rational creature, he knows that death is inevitable. He stands in a relationship to death because of his awareness of death's inevitability. Man's relationship to his death thus becomes one of the many relationships which constitute his life. Knowledge of death's inevitability is thus one case of knowledge among the many cases, which, when taken together, have their basis in the fact that man has the capacity for knowledge. Is this the case?

Or is it in fact quite the opposite? Many would argue that the experience of negation which death effects upon life is more fundamental than the experience of thinking; that the most painfully astonishing thing about the experience of death is that it excludes the act of thinking. When everything is one, when everything fits perfectly together and is at one with itself, then no mind is at work. Thinking occurs when things do not fit together. This is why Aristotle said that philosophy begins in wonder and astonishment.[12] Is not the experience of death and of death's inevitability somehow similar to this elemental wonder, the wonder which estranges us from the object and from which thought then begins to emerge?

The Platonic understanding of the death of Socrates and of this conception of the relationship between death and knowledge was not only of some considerable importance for the Western spiritual tradition; it imprinted itself indelibly upon it. Here, death is not understood simply as one object among others, nor even as the primary object of knowledge. It is the one real object of all knowledge. The identity between 'memento mori' and 'gnothi sauton' means that as far as knowledge of any kind is concerned, it is a question of knowing oneself as one who will and must die. Death is thus

regarded as the one event which can effect knowledge itself.
For death is the object of knowledge, the true object of all
knowledge precisely and only because it is the event which
sets one free for pure knowledge. In this sense death is
deprived of its negative aspect. With death there appears that
which endures and remains, that which is of value because it
endures. Thus knowledge of death is self-knowledge. That
which perishes with death deserves to perish: the body. That
which endures is the true self, the soul, whose real essence
and function is: to know. For these reasons 'memento mori'
and 'gnothi sauton' are identical (and vice versa), for the
person who has self-knowledge knows that he is the being
destined for knowledge and that through death he will attain
his destiny. The reason why the living should remember
that they will die is that in death man comes wholly to
himself. The 'memento mori' is not meant to overawe and
subdue. It is a demand which gives life promise. It is
a promise which is fulfilled in terms of the increase in
knowledge which men can experience in their lives. As the
object of knowledge death is an event which itself augments
knowledge. Death thus casts no shadow, but rather light.

The way for this understanding of death was prepared by
Orphism and the Pythagoreans. However, from a historical
point of view it is worth noting that this positive understanding
of death was by no means self-evident in the Greek world.
Lessing was of the opinion that the Greeks had wholly
reconciled themselves to death.[13] But the opposite was true.
Schelling's view was that sadness at life's transience penetrated
the artistic works of ancient Greece like a 'sweet poison'. The
more beautiful the world, the more terrifying was death. This
is why in Homer's 'Odyssey' the doomed Achilles restrains
Odysseus when he tries to comfort him by praising death: . . .
'spare me your praise of death, my lord Odysseus. Put me on
earth again, and I would rather be a serf in the house of
some landless man, with little enough for himself to live on,
than king of all these dead men that have done with life.'[14]

This was the typical attitude of the Greek to death. It gave cause either for resignation, or at best, cause to profit in the enjoyment of this transient life.

The philosophy which is derived from the death of Socrates is quite different from this. It made of death something positive. Death does not negate; it sets free. It marks a fulfilment rather than an ending. It signifies happiness rather than pain. This is why swans sing before they die—'more loudly and more sweetly'—not because of sadness, but for joy, because they will die to Apollo, the god of song, their lord (84E).[15] In death Socrates excels the swans. Apollo, the god of the Delphic oracle, was also his lord. His swan-song thus becomes a song of praise to death.

That death is not only the object of knowledge but also influences knowing itself is one of the acknowledged facts of the Platonic interpretation of the death of Socrates. However, Plato has drawn the sting of negation from death. Since the real meaning of death is so closely connected with knowing (as purifying and augmenting the self), death is evaluated in a *positive* way within the context of existence.

Despite any apparent similarities, the Platonic understanding of death may be radically contrasted with another view of the relationship between death and knowledge. It can be illustrated with the help of a few statements from Hegel's *Phenomenology of Mind*. Hegel calls death 'the energy of thought'. This is something which could also be understood in wholly Platonic terms. However, Hegel understands this energy of thought with its source in death as 'the monstrous power of the negative'. Its negative character is something from which it can never be free. 'Death . . . is the most terrible thing, and to keep and hold fast to what is dead demands the greatest force of all.' Death is the source of knowledge to the extent that it puts an end to the 'familiar'. For Hegel, a clear distinction must be made between that with which we are merely familiar and that which we really know. 'What we are "familiar with" is not intelligently known, just for the reason that it is "familiar"'. As the familiar the familiar itself must rather be negated in order for it to be really known. 'It is the commonest form of self-deception, and a deception of other people as well, to assume something to be familiar, and give assent to it on that very account.' One goes on talking backwards and forwards about the familiar. But this results in nothing new and certainly in no new knowledge: 'Knowledge of that sort, with all its talk, never gets from the spot.' Knowledge can only be attained when the familiar presents itself in a new light and is thereby seen to be no longer merely familiar. Once it is no longer recognised as the familiar it is distinguished from itself. As the familiar it thus becomes unreal and so passes away. That the familiar as such should vanish by the negation involved in separation is due to the activity of the understanding. 'The action of separating the elements is the exercise of the force of *understanding*, the most astonishing and greatest of all powers, or rather the absolute power.' The power which the understanding possesses consists precisely in its capacity to confront the reality of negation, to look death in the face and thus arrive at genuine knowledge. Knowing, therefore, is not merely a matter of describing reality; it is 'to hold fast to what is dead'. Thus apart from 'the Golgotha of the Spirit', mind is not mind. 'Beauty, powerless and helpless, hates understanding, because the latter extracts from it what it cannot perform', namely, 'to hold fast what is dead'. 'But the life of mind is not one that shuns death, and keeps clear of destruction; it endures its death and in death maintains its being. It only wins to its truth when it finds itself in utter desolation. It is this mighty power, not by being a positive which turns away from the negative, as when we say of anything it is nothing or it is false, and, being then done with it, pass off to something else; on the contrary, mind is this power only by looking the negative in the face and dwelling with it.'[16]

This is also a 'commentatio mortis': but it is a thinking about death of a different kind. In this case also, death is the model for knowledge. But the death which here must be confronted is not death as involving release (of the soul from the body) and purification. It is death as involving division and devastation. 'Death, if this is what we care to call such an unreality, is the most terrible thing.' Here, death's negativity is not disputed. Nor is there any attempt to avoid it. Its pain is not explained away nor euphemised. It is to be borne and suffered. Only in this way can one attain to knowledge, and this knowledge consists in giving a future to that which is past and new being to that which has been ravaged. On this theory of knowledge, knowledge is thoroughly *historical* in the sense that knowing and the content of knowledge have and make a history. Knowledge by acquaintance must first vanish in order for the object to be truly known. The theory of the historicity of knowledge (of the spirit) is derived from this insight into death's *negative* character which, at the point of its utmost intensity receives positive significance. This formulation of the way in which the relationship between death and knowledge is determined is opposed to the Platonic view. It is a view which would not have been possible apart from the understanding of death which is disclosed in and through the death of Jesus Christ.

The death of Socrates suggests that the deadly poison is a health-giving medicine. Socrates greeted death with a swan-song. When Jesus died he uttered a cry. The swan-song announced the return to God. Jesus cried: My God, my God, why hast thou forsaken me? This is to look the negative in the face.

And yet it is precisely the death of Jesus which is proclaimed as salvation.

The de-Platonising of Christianity—a theological task
Through death to immortality, 'per aspera ad astra'—this is the ruling conception which has dominated a platonised Christianity. A de-platonised Christianity must break with it. For hundreds of years the mosaic in the National Museum in

Rome could be unreservedly regarded as Christian. The
identification of 'gnothi sauton' with 'memento mori' seemed
to correspond exactly to a text which is frequently quoted
and used as a sermon text: '(Lord) teach us to remember
that we must die (to number our days) that we may get a
heart of wisdom' (Ps. 90: 12). Here also, with the recognition
that one must die, one may attain to wisdom. However, the very
fact that we must *pray* for this insight should induce a certain
scepticism. Here, self-knowledge and knowledge of death are
mediated by Another. That this Other must first of all teach
man to 'count his days' shows just how much the men of the
Old Testament resist this insight. He cannot attain to it by
himself. However, in addition to this, the Old Testament,
apart from which the New Testament would not be what
it is, represents the most rigorous and effective objection to the
understanding of death which is rooted in the Platonic
conception of the death of Socrates. Plato's solution to the
question of death cannot be the Christian one.

Let us now conclude this part of our discussion. We have
dealt with 'the enigma of death'. We have attempted to show
that the facts about death which often appear to us to be
enigmatic, can and should be illuminated. In the following
discussion we shall deal with 'the mystery of death'. To set
aside the enigmas which surround a thing does not mean that it
has ceased to be mysterious. There are things and circumstances, persons and events, which become more mysterious
the better one understands them. Riddles can be solved. The
mysterious remains mysterious even when we have knowledge
of it. 'The world should not be enigmatic . . . But should
it be without mystery? Only the most incurable bore can
say that the world is without mystery. Whoever maintains
that mystery is not part of experience has not yet begun
to open himself to experience' (Bernet).[17]

The theological answer to the question of death which
follows seeks to divest the event of death of its enigmatic
character. The discipline of theology brings death within the

dimension of the rational. In the light of the Gospel theology can throw light upon the question of death. But having gained some light on the problem, and having clarified the problem of death itself, neither the person so enlightened nor the question of death itself lose their mysterious character within the dimension of rationality. To understand that man must die, that death is most alien to our being and yet at the same time so essentially part of us, can only mean that death's enigmas should be resolved in such a way that its true mystery may appear. Theological talk of death can therefore seek to be nothing other than an attempt to introduce and confront us with the mystery of death. In this connection we are guided by the statements about death which have come down to us in the Bible. Ever anew we must respond to these statements and ever anew we must be responsible to them.

PART TWO

THE MYSTERY OF DEATH

4. The Death of the Sinner
(Death as the Wages of Sin)

Biblical views on death
Old Testament attitudes to death
New Testament attitudes to death

5. The Death of Jesus Christ
(Death as God's Passion)

The death of Jesus as the event of salvation
The life of Jesus and faith in God
Jesus' death and faith in Jesus
Death and God

6. The Death of Death
(Death as this Present Life made Eternal)

The two dimensions of the biblical understanding of death
Death and time—the hope of faith
Death and equality—a socio-political consideration
Death and anxiety—the obligation of faith

Chapter Four

The Death of the Sinner

(Death as the Wages of Sin)

Biblical views on death

There is no one agreed view of death in the Bible. In almost all the biblical writings each of the different interpretations of death has certain characteristics in common. For example, the evaluation of the fact that man must die is a predominantly negative one. However, such common characteristics cannot conceal the fact that different understandings of death are to be found in the Bible. What we have is rather like a history of the different approaches to an understanding of the question of death. Like every real history, this history is not an abstract construction. This means that within it there are certain contradictions.

One contrast or contradiction within the long history of the biblical approach to the problem of death is quite fundamental. With regard to Christian faith in God it is of the utmost importance. Within a context of profound agreement, a contrast begins to emerge and can be recognised between Old Testament attitudes to dying, and Old Testament conceptions of death, and those which are to be found in the New Testament. There are factual grounds for this contrast. It is not only that conceptions and views of death and attitudes to death have changed. Something, as it were, has happened to death itself. A new attitude to death and a new understanding of death have become possible.

Christian faith makes the claim that something has happened to death itself. It is precisely this which constitutes the peculiar meaning of the death of Jesus Christ upon which faith is based, which faith proclaims and upon which it also reflects. Faith in the resurrection is the confession that with the death of Jesus Christ death is no longer the same. It implies that something has changed with regard to the fact that man must die. The fact that we have a New Testament at all is not unrelated to this. We can safely say that the ultimate basis for the decisive differences not only between the Old Testament and New Testament conceptions of death, but also for the difference between the Old Testament and the New Testament themselves is the death of Jesus Christ. Much more than their profound agreements therefore, contrast and difference signify that both testaments belong essentially together. For if something has really happened to death itself through the death of Jesus Christ, and if it also affects the fact that man cannot live and at the same time avoid death's inevitability, then it will be seen that it is because of this event that both testaments belong much more essentially together in their differing and contrasting attitudes to the problem and the fact of death than would several fully harmonious conceptions of death deriving from different historical periods.

In the following section, therefore, we shall attempt to acquaint ourselves with the most important Old Testament statements on this matter. Against this background, and with the help of the New Testament texts, we shall then examine the meaning of the death of Jesus.

What the biblical texts have to say about death can first of all be distinguished from the many profound religious and secular views on this subject, both old and new, by the fact that although the question of death is given decisive importance, it is not of all-decisive importance. That our entire life should be a 'commentatio mortis' is not an attitude which can be defended on biblical grounds. Nor is the demand that we should count our days or the parable of the rich farmer to be understood in this way.

The Bible of course leaves us in no doubt that death is terrifying and even repugnant. However, to call death the real inspirational genius of philosophy (Schopenhauer), is something which without regret can and must be left to the philosophers if we are to orientate ourselves toward the Bible.[1] The question of death, reflection upon it, and existential concern about the end of earthly life certainly touches upon that which is ultimate. But it is not the 'hub of the wheel'. An answer to the question of death, some glimpse behind this dark veil, would by no means provide us with a magic key which could unlock every door. Why is there anything at all and not nothing? To this basic philosophical question a biblical consideration of death cannot and will not provide an answer. Faith cannot take death quite so seriously.

For the fact is that faith gives an incomparable primacy to life so that death, even in its most relentless rigour, (something of which faith is also certainly most painfully aware), cannot catch up with it. Death, as Paul says, is the wages of sin. But the Apostle immediately goes on to say—and this is the most important point: 'but the free gift of God is eternal life in Jesus Christ our Lord' (Rom. 6: 23). It may well be that philosophy is indebted to death. It may well be the case also that philosophy is no more than philosophy of death. A theology of death can be no more than a chapter of theology, albeit an important and decisive one. For theology, as it always has been and is, is talk of God. Faith will find itself unable to speak of God unless it can also speak of death. But talk of God is much more than talk of death. Theology does not owe its existence to the fact that we must die, and it is something other than simply a theology of death.

Old Testament attitudes to death
In accordance with our methodological standpoint, it has been suggested that our questions about death should be set within the context of life and within the framework of the attitudes to death which men adopt. This is exactly how the Old Testament texts approach the problem. Hebrew man knows death as one of life's tests. Thus in any attempt to come

to an understanding of death, we must also attempt to
understand the Old Testament attitude to life.

(*a*) *Life as the highest good.* In the Old Testament we find
references to death quite apart from any corresponding
references to death. The Israelites found themselves confronted
with death at every step. The death-rate was extremely high.
Thus it is easy to understand why life, man's earthly existence
between birth and death, was held in such high esteem.
Life is a good; it is the highest of goods. A long life, a fulfilled
life, (Gen. 15: 15; Judges 8: 32; Job 42: 17 etc.), life with an
assured posterity, (Ps. 127, 128 etc.), are the best gifts
that God can give. Life is a blessing, death a curse (Deut. 30: 19).
To have life is to have joy at life, and to live joyfully is rightly
to enjoy God (Schunack).[2] Thus to those who seek God there
is the promise of life. The question of life becomes not so much
a matter of bread and other means of subsistence, but of the
Word of God (Deut. 8: 3). Behind this is the notion that
God Himself is the Living One (Deut. 5: 26; 2 Kings 19: 4;
Ps. 42: 3), that He is the fountain of life (Ps. 36: 9).

This makes it easier for us to understand the relatively
late text: 'thy steadfast love is better than life' (Ps. 63: 3).
This is one of the rare instances where it is suggested that
for Israel, grace surpasses life. Up to this point, grace and
life were understood to be on an equal footing. Grace was
life. This distinction between grace and life can be understood
in the light of the fact that grace may be interpreted as
involving participation in God Himself, the Lord of life.
Such an interpretation is justified in view of those contexts
which refer to a vision of God, a quite exceptional event in
which participation in God's very being is granted by God
Himself in such a way that the soul of the person who is
granted this vision of God is 'feasted as with marrow and fat'
(Ps. 63: 5).

If God, the Living One, is the fountain of life, then no-one
can have life apart from Him. Life is not some mythological,

independent reality, nor is it something which man can set out to search after, as, for example, in the ancient Babylonian Gilgamesh epic. The tree of life in paradise (Gen. 2 and 3) is understood to have no value in itself. It is God who disposes over it; He ordains its worth and function, not man (Gen. 3: 22). God gives life and takes it again (Ps. 104: 29ff.; Job 34: 14f.). Just as He has given man the breath of life in order that he may live at all (Gen. 2: 7), he also allots to him a life-span, (Gen. 6: 3). Man's time is in God's hand (Ps. 31: 15; 139: 16). Thus as far as the Old Testament is concerned, man's life is a gift. It is not his own possession.

This is something to which we must pay particular attention. For this means after all that that which is closest to man, the very ground of his existence and his being is not something which belongs to him. It means that his life, that which is most his own, is nevertheless not his own. To put it briefly and pointedly, man's life is not at his own disposal. Even though he has dominion over the earth (Gen. 1: 28), he is not his own lord. However, not to be one's own master does not imply some anthropological lack. It is rather an indication that man can live *only in relationships*, that since he stands at a distance from himself, he cannot be related to himself without at the same time standing in a relationship to God.

Human life is thus not wholly devoid of promise. For man cannot be truly himself without at the same time standing 'outside himself' before God. Whether he is aware of it or not, or whether he even cares to be aware of it, man receives his true self from beyond himself. He cannot come to himself without moving beyond himself. One of the best indications of man's openness beyond himself is the fact of the linguistic character of his existence. We relate to the world by listening to it. We open ourselves beyond the world and ourselves through speech. However, if the self is related to God and the world as always before us, and if this relationship exists quite apart from anything we actually do, then for our part the task becomes that of relating ourselves to God and our world in our concrete behaviour and conduct. If he wishes to maintain a relationship to the world, and if he wants to attain genuine selfhood, that is to say, if he wants to live, then man must attend to God by listening. Thus: 'Hear, that your soul may live' (Isa. 55: 3). For it is by listening to God's law that man is related to the source of all the relationships within which life can alone be lived. It is by listening that man most fittingly responds to the relationship in which he stands to God and to the relationships within which his life is lived. He who is upright in his relationships is just and is declared just by the priests (Lev. 3: 5; Neh. 9: 29; Hab. 2: 4; Ezra 18: 5–9). And he who is just shall live. In more general terms, in the Old Testament Wisdom literature, quite apart from any cultic presuppositions, the promise to those who 'make their ears attentive to wisdom' (Prov. 2: 2), is a long life and years of abundance (Prov. 3: 1f.; 9: 11).

Of the person who does not live uprightly in his relationships and who for this reason cannot be declared just, it is said that he should die. This is not some new point of view, but the same thing expressed in a negative way. Similarly, as the logical alternative, the way which is opposed to the way of wisdom is the way that leads to death (Prov. 2: 18f.; 5: 5 etc.). We shall return to this question in due course.

(b) *Life in the face of death.* Of course death also comes to those who do seek God, to those who listen to his Word and to those who really follow the way of wisdom. Even for the most pious in Israel death was something which in the long run could not be evaded. In the end, all men die (Ps. 89: 48f.). This is an experience which Israel cannot escape. It was one of the most bitter tests of faith. The melancholy preacher gave poignant expression to this struggle: 'How the wise man dies just like the fool! So I hated life . . .' (Eccl. 2: 16f.).

However, other similar difficult tests of faith do not necessarily lead to such resignation. These bitter struggles are meant to strengthen the faith of Israel; that in standing the test, faith may become strong enough to value the present relationship to God far above any alternative between life and death. Once again, man's relationship to God is seen to be more valuable than the supreme good of earthly life.

There are a few Old Testament texts which hint at this attitude in the faith of the people of Israel. One is the statement to which we have already referred: 'Thy steadfast love is better than life' (Ps. 63: 4). The text in which the worshipper refers to God as 'my portion in the land of the living' (Ps. 142: 5), is perhaps another. As long as no doctrine of human immortality is teased out of it, then under this heading we may also include Psalm 73. Faced with the fact that the godless flourish, the writer comforts himself with the thought that a terrible death must await them. The upright, on the other hand, having lived their life in communion with God, will be separated from them and 'received to glory' (v. 24). Here it is difficult to see how any end other than death can be conceivable. However, a great deal will depend upon the way in which v. 26 is interpreted: 'My flesh and my heart may fail, but God is the strength of my heart and my portion for ever . . . ' This means that it is by *grace*, that the man who lives in the awareness that his true self is with God is drawn away from himself toward God both in life and in death. This is why he has 'made the Lord God (his) refuge' (v. 28). On the other hand, those who trust in themselves withdraw from the relationship to God in which they have always stood and the relationship is broken. Their end is the most terrible of contradictions because they have been untrue to themselves. In being untrue to God, they are even more profoundly untrue to themselves and so are shattered upon a rock of self-contradiction. 'For lo, those who are far from thee shall perish; thou dost put an end to those who are false to thee' (v. 27). And finally, Job 19: 25–27 must also be included among those texts which insist upon the excellence of man's present relationship to the God who is the fountain of life, the bond which surpasses in value the alternatives of life and death. In

the certainty that his 'redeemer' lives, and that he shall
(again?) appear on earth, the defeated and ill-treated Job is
confident that he 'shall see God' (v. 26). We are not to think
here of a resurrection of the dead. The dead have 'gone
down' and do not return (Job 7: 9f., 21; 10: 21f.; 16: 22).
This statement amounts to no more than the trust that as far
as Job's wretched condition is concerned, the last word has
not yet been spoken.

These texts which we have just discussed hint at some
attempt to move beyond the either-or of life and death. But
they amount to no more than tentative approaches. The
view of the Old Testament as a rule is that life is the supreme
good. We must now examine this in connection with what the
Old Testament has to say about *death*. It will be of considerable
help if we devote our attention first of all to what appear to be
the more external factors of Israelite custom and practice.
This will enable us to come to a better understanding of the
Hebrew's attitude to dying and to death.

(c) *Attitudes to age, to dying and to death*. For Israel, death is a
process which is quite naturally bound up with the process of
ageing. Although it was something which frequently occurred,
an early death is an untimely death. The infant-mortality rate
was high. Thus it is with pride that a father can say: 'sons have
I reared and brought up' (Isa. 1: 2, the reference in this case
is to God). He who grows old with honour is visibly blessed. The
view of the Greeks that 'those whom the gods love they leave
to die young' is quite foreign to the Old Testament.

In the midst of his struggles, the man who is distressed
beyond measure is more likely to express the despairing wish
that he had never been born at all. In his misery, Job wishes
that he had been buried in secret like a miscarried child
(Job 3: 16, and compare also the melancholy view of the
Preacher in Eccl. 3: 6). More in keeping with the Old
Testament as a whole is that it is this which should be wished
upon Israel's enemies (Ps. 58: 8). This would confirm the view

that the untimely end of a life—ending in this case before it
begins—is indeed a bad end.

To die in the midst of life is to suffer the end of a fool
(Jer. 17: 11, with regard to the man who falsely gains riches).
Man's life must as it were become ripe for death, and it is for
this reason that sudden death is also regarded as something
bad (Ps. 90: 5–6). 'We must all die, we are like water spilt on
the ground, which cannot be gathered up again, but God will
not take away (life) . . .' if there is no reason for doing so
(2 Sam. 14: 14; see also Job 34: 12–15). The blessed of the
Lord die 'in a good old age' (Gen. 25: 8; Jud. 8: 32;
1 Chr. 29: 28). When a ripe old age is reached, then it is time
for death. It then becomes clear that dying is the way of all the
earth (1 Kings 2: 2), a way upon which man cannot wish not
to go. Old and full of years (Gen. 25: 8; 35: 29; Job 42: 17;
1 Chr. 23: 1; 2 Chr. 24: 15)—man *can* die in this way; thus
the necessity of death at the same time becomes a possibility
which man does not exclude. Still, it costs less to support an old
man than it does to support a six-year old boy, and at 60 a
woman's economic worth begins to decrease, though not so
rapidly as that of a man. ('For what value has an old man?
And how valuable it is to have in the household an aged
mother or aunt'—These are points raised by Ludwig Köhler).[3]

The old person estimates his worth also in the light of death.
Old age with its ailments and troubles usually hampers the
enjoyment of life. The capacity for life decreases (though not in
the case of Moses who is regarded as an exception, Deut.
34: 7). The eyes grow dim (Gen. 27: 1; 48: 10; 1 Sam. 3: 2;
1 Kings 14: 4, though again, this does not apply to Moses,
Deut. 34: 7). People have to sit because their legs are no
longer strong enough to support them (Zech. 8: 4). One cannot
keep warm, and it is for this reason that a young maiden is made
to share the old king David's bed (1 Kings 1: 1–4). For man,
this is the time when 'the evil days come, and the years draw
nigh when you will say, "I have no pleasure in them"'
(Eccl. 12: 1). The expression 'full of days' can also be under-

stood in this way (Köhler).[4] Man is prepared. Death holds no terrors for him.

The *dead* are buried immediately. The nature of the climate is such that it hastens decay. Arrangements for burial must therefore be made quickly. It is the relatives who make the arrangements. Abraham buries his wife Sarah (Gen. 23: 19), and he in turn is buried by his sons (Gen. 25: 9). 'A man's kinsman' (Amos 6: 10) is the one responsible for the burial. The 'funeral' is usually an interment. Cremation, on the other hand, is less common. Cremation is reserved as a degrading treatment for criminals, and above all as a punishment for fornication (Gen. 38: 24; Lev. 20: 14; 21: 9). As a punishment of the living, cremation was required not because of the pain involved in undergoing such a death, but rather because by burning the criminal, burial might thereby be wholly denied him. He would thus be consigned to utter nothingness (Quell).[5] Stoning serves the same purpose as cremation: the person to be punished in this way 'would be covered with stones so that nothing of him was left there' (Köhler).[6]

To be refused burial was regarded as extremely grave. To be offered as fodder to the dogs or the birds meant that a distinction between man and beast could no longer be made: 'the burial of an ass' (Jer. 22: 19). The Jewish interpreters of the Old Testament give warnings against dying at sea and of thus having no grave.

As a rule, the burial-places were to be found outside the settled areas. Only children or princes were from time to time buried in the house. Normally, the bodies were buried in a city of the dead, a necropolis set at some distance from the dwelling places of the living. The graves of the well-to-do were different from those of the poor. While people of few means were probably buried in graves in the earth (see the expression 'graves of the common people' 2 Kings 23: 6), the rich were buried in rock tombs of a more distinguished and permanent nature. Not being subject to decay these survive through the ages and so become welcome objects for the archaeologist's spade. In early times coffins were not used. They come into use only in the Hellenistic period.

In Old Testament times, the bodies were laid on benches placed against the right and left hand walls and on the wall opposite the entrance. Here a man would be 'gathered to his fathers'. Room was made for other members of the family by later removing the bones from the benches and laying them out in a common grave which was usually to be found in the corner of the tomb. Burial inscriptions with the names of the dead are unknown at this time. The name is something which belongs to the living. And the name of the dead person can live on only through the living.

Setting aside for the moment these considerations with regard to burial customs, this is something which deserves special attention. In terms of language itself, in the consequent linguistic tradition in which he is represented by his name, the dead person lives on. In this sense there is the possibility of survival beyond death. Historical remembrance *may* thus help to ease the problem of death in that those who succeed me will, historically speaking, recall my death as the death of *another*. However, this possibility of historical recollection may also have a negative effect: the wicked person, the evil-doer, may be remembered as 'a proverb, and a byword' (Deut. 28: 37). As a rule, however, after a certain time, any remembrance of the dead person is extinguished and his name is forgotten. Even of God it can be said that the time comes when he no longer holds the dead in remembrance. However, God's capacity for remembrance is not like man's. When he no longer *remembers* the dead person, this does not mean that he has forever *forgotten* him. This is a point which is firmly emphasised in the New Testament: the man whom God has called by his name (see also Isa. 49: 1), belongs to him forever; 'you are mine' (Isa. 43: 1). It was precisely in this, in God's verbal intercourse with man, that Luther found grounds for hope in eternal life: 'Whenever and to whom God speaks, whether in wrath or in grace, that man is of a certainty immortal. The Person of God who thus speaks, and his Word, announce that we are such creatures that God wants to speak with us eternally and immortally.'[7]

But let us now gather some further information about burial customs! Individual burial was something which came into being only with the arrival of the Roman-Hellenistic period (single tombs, coffins, burial inscriptions). However in every period different kinds of gifts were buried along with the body, 'items connected with daily life such as clay containers, clay lamps, receptacles for ointment, jewellery, weapons' (Noth).[8] In the grave, the dead have thus not simply become nothing. They are still present in a way which is similar to the mode of existence of the living. They dwell there: 'the grave is a dwelling' (Quell). But this 'dwelling' is not part of the world. Like desert and ocean, the grave is rather not-world.

In the Old Testament, the dead do not simply 'go down to the pit' (Isa. 38: 18; Ps. 28: 1; 30: 14 etc.). The dead also go to *Sheol,* a 'region' inexactly described as 'the realm of the dead'. Sheol is beneath. To Sheol man goes down (Isa. 7: 11), never to return (Job 7: 9f.; 2 Sam. 12: 23). It is the place of going down (Job 26: 6; 28: 22; Prov. 15: 11); without light (Job 10: 21); a place of stillness (Ps. 94: 17; 115: 17). There, distinctions are meaningless (Job 3: 19); they are recognised, but only in order to note their unimportance. It is joyless and somnolent. 'All mental activity is at an end' (Quell).[9] The existence of the dead person, the life which is no more, has a benumbed, ghostly quality. The dead assembled in Sheol are dead in the sense that they remain transfixed in attitude to the life that once was theirs. 'This assembly of those who once lived, of husks empty of life . . . is like the figures in a waxworks . . . Once dead, a man is dead forever, "till the heavens are no more he will not awake, or be roused out of his sleep" ' (Job 14: 12) (Maag).[10] The dead are 'in the land of forgetfulness' (Ps. 88: 12). It is a comfortless expression.

These notions of the dead in the grave and in Sheol are to be found side by side unharmonised. Such conceptions are not original to the faith of Israel. They belong to the wider religious-historical background of the Old Testament. As such they were to give rise to some difficult problems as far as faith in the God of Israel was concerned.

Problems were to emerge, for example, in connection with *mourning*. Once the dead have been buried as quickly as possible there follows a period of mourning when certain customs are observed. There is frequent weeping and lamentation. In this regard, like mourning itself, weeping is not primarily an expression of subjective emotion. The austere sensitivity of David's lamentation over Saul and Jonathan is much more the exception in this respect. 'For the Hebrew, mourning was a much more tangible thing. When Joseph and his brothers held a mourning for his father for seven days, this does not mean that they wept for seven days because their minds could not become reconciled to their father's death . . . In order to lament the dead the bereaved will assemble for seven days in succession at some time in the morning and possibly in the evening as well and weep together just as devout Jews still do today' (Köhler).[11] Weeping is thus not so much the involuntary expression of subjective emotion. 'The Hebrew can weep at will'. And this is the custom when someone dies.

To participate in rites of mourning is to become unclean. But this defilement is necessary if one is to take leave of the dead, 'for even the dearest person, when once he is dead, is a member of another world, the realm of death, and therefore uncanny, and something to be avoided, "unclean". It is thus that the real meaning of the observances and customs of mourning may be explained. They were settlements with the dead, methods of release from them' (Köhler).[12]

(*d*) *Death's ambivalence*. Although the Old Testament rarely has anything good to say about it, death, in its negativity, is not to be seen as the direct counterbalance to life. They are not to be regarded as standing on equal terms. Death of course does mark the end of human life. It constitutes a continual threat to life and to this extent it is a decided evil. Death is an evil, yet it comes only together with a mercy which is given by God. Life itself is also the condition for the possibility of death, and death must be accepted along with life. 'Shall we receive good at the hand of God, and shall we not receive evil?' (Job 2: 10). In principle at least then, to pray to God for protection from an untimely end, or to save one from mortal affliction, is not to rebel against death. As long as one lives one has the will to live. And to die 'old and full of years' is the sign of a blessed life. If death then comes, such a man has nevertheless lived; he has truly lived. And this is an advantage which cannot be reversed even by death. It is indeed something to have lived and to have been.

For Israel, death's power has its limits. It is subordinate to the power of God. Israel's faith is also decidedly allergic to the powerful and widespread interest to be found among neighbouring religions in the despotic power of death and of the dead. The mourning rites of other religions were resisted (Deut. 14: 1; 26: 14). It was undesirable to consult the dead (Lev. 19: 31; Deut. 18: 11). Notions of the process of dying, conceptions of the mode of existence (or non-existence) of the dead, of the grave and of the realm of the dead therefore diverge. It is characteristic that there was clearly no theological reason for attempting to harmonise these divergent views. The relationship of the Israelites to death was unquestionably reserved.

There are certain theological motives behind this reserve. Strangely enough, the reason for it stems in the first instance from two apparently contradictory points of view. On the one hand, God's dominion over death prevents it from having any independent significance. It is *God* who kills and brings to life (1 Sam. 2: 6). It is *he* who returns man to the dust (Ps. 90: 3). On the other hand, however, faith in God as the fountain of all life requires that one should adopt an attitude of religious reserve toward death. Israel's God is the God of the living, not of the dead. The dead are cut off from his hand (Ps. 88: 6).

Bodies are unclean and must be removed from the sphere of the divine (Lev. 21:1; Num. 19:16; Deut. 21:23). The realm of the dead is set at a distance from God. Israel's faith had to respect the distance between God and the realm of death by maintaining a corresponding reserve toward any attempt to encourage a religious interest in death as such.

It is on the basis of this that the problem of a theological understanding of death is really raised. This reserve toward death which was so characteristic of the faith of Israel does not mean that Israel had somehow pushed death aside; nor does it demonstrate that as far as Israel was concerned, a theological understanding of death was impossible. Quite the contrary! It is precisely faith's reserve toward death, and toward the all-important doctrine of 'immortality' (which is so significant to religions in every age), which itself gives pregnant expression to a theological understanding of death. This is what the Old Testament has to offer. As far as any Old Testament theology of death is concerned, death itself has in the end no independent role. Putting it bluntly, we may say that as an *isolated* phenomenon it simply does not exist. To die is human. Death is thus not something which can be isolated and abstracted from man's life. Death means precisely that it is men who die. In the faith of Israel there is therefore to this extent a tendency to demythologise death. In the New Testament this is something which works itself out in a quite radical way.

It is not that death has somehow been rendered innocuous. Men die, their lives have an end. Only in exceptionally note-worthy cases is this end understood as life's fulfilment. Nowhere in the Old Testament is it disputed that death can be exactly this: an end which marks the fulfilment of a man's life. There are sufficient further grounds to support the view that death could be experienced in this way and that this was how it was intended by God: 'You shall come to your grave in ripe old age, as a shock of grain comes up to the threshing floor in its season' (Job 5:26). This was how the patriarchs were under-stood to have died. To die at a ripe old age was something

which they could simply take for granted (Gen. 27: 2;
46: 30; 48: 21; 50: 24). Every man *could* die in this way. In
reality, however, it is different.

In reality man *must* die, for it is not within his own power to
fulfil himself and he cannot bring his life to a peaceful end.
In reality man must die, although—and in fact because—he
cannot die. That is the meaning of death and that is what
makes it so bitter: we cannot die and yet must.

In reality, death is something different from what it could be.
In reality death is unnatural. In reality it is a curse—a curse
which man himself of course invites from God. In the Old
Testament, death's real misery can be understood only against
the background of Israel's relationship to God. It is a relationship grounded in the distinction between God's holiness and
man's utter lack of holiness. In itself this can be a deadly
contrast. Whoever sees the holy God may die (Jud. 13: 22;
Isa. 6: 5; Exod. 33: 20). Death is the result once the relationship to God is broken.

Of course it is only in concrete specific cases that death is
seen to have something to do with the broken God-relationship.
In more general terms death is basically regarded as a
punishment only in the creation story: 'but of the tree of the
knowledge of good and evil you shall not eat, for in the day
that you eat of it you shall die' (Gen. 2: 17, cf. Gen. 3: 19).
The drastic curtailment of man's length of days is also seen as
a punishment (Gen. 6: 3). That death is the wages of sin is
something which is asserted only in the New Testament, and
there this is viewed from within the wider context of victory
over death. Nevertheless, throughout the entire Old Testament,
death is specifically related to man's guilt, the guilt which he
must bear throughout his life and which he cannot explain.
Death does not merely cast its shadow over human life. It is
rather that the shadow cast by death is no more than the
haunting primordial shadow, now extended and magnified,
which our life casts upon our ending.

It is vitally important that we should be as clear as possible about this particular biblical point of view. It is a generally accepted anthropological fact that death poses a radical problem for the life we live. However, as we live it, life also makes a radical problem of death. The fact that we *make* death the supreme problem, that we *make* it the one 'aporia', the real 'cul-de-sac' of our lives points to the genuinely biblical aspect of this generally accepted anthropological truth. The significance of this may be expressed quite pointedly: in the course of our lives it is what we make of life that causes death to become the uncanny power which threatens not only the individual, but whole communities and even nations.

This is why the hand of Sheol extends beyond its boundaries to reach into the midst of man's happy life! (Ps. 49: 14–15; 89: 48). *This* is why death catches man like a fish in a net (Eccl. 9: 12), and *entangles* him (2 Sam. 22: 6; Ps. 18: 6). *This* is why Sheol opens its mouth and its jaws to the multitude, 'and the nobility of Jerusalem go down, her throng and he who exults in her' (Isa. 5: 14). *This* is why death can be compared with man's avarice. Like death it is *insatiable*. It gathers and unites all men and nations (Hab. 2: 5; Prov. 27: 20). *This* is why death constantly approaches life from all sides and threatens to destroy it, bringing it to a sudden and terrifying end (Ps. 73: 19). *This* is why death poses a constant threat to life.

This is why it is so. Death therefore, does not have to mean that we cannot die yet must. It does not have to be a threat, for it can be a peaceful end. It does not have to be contrary to nature, for it could be natural. It does not mean that it must come prematurely, in an untimely way, or at an evil time (Prov. 9: 12); it could occur at a time which is fitting. It does not necessarily have to imply a sudden break with everything, for in the true sense it can be a genuine ending.

We are not dealing with some essentially unrealistic possibility or some abstract notion. This is a genuine possibility. The evidence for it is that death in this sense has in fact occurred. The death of the patriarchs is a good example.

The awareness of the possibility of death in this sense is briefly but beautifully expressed in the text which we have already quoted from the book of Job: 'You shall come to the grave in ripe old age, as a shock of grain comes up to the threshing floor in its season' (Job 5: 26). Requests for deliverance from death and thanksgivings for deliverance received at least give indirect indication that the evil of death does not have to be man's end. The texts of the Old Testament which speak of deliverance from death never suggest that God protects man from death itself. Man is however delivered from the concrete danger of death, and he is protected from untimely death at an 'evil time'. To be delivered from death means that one's life is prolonged so that the number of one's days may be fulfilled (Exod. 23: 26). In the end, for Israel, the longed for future time of salvation in the new Jerusalem was pictured as a time when there would be no old man who had not fulfilled his days— that is, who was not ripe for death (see Isa. 65: 20; Zech. 8: 4). Death can therefore be something other than a curse.

Death therefore clearly has this peculiar ambivalence. We experience it and judge it entirely from the point of view of the life we actually live, as life goes either well or badly with us. And this is exactly why the death which man cannot die yet must is not peaceful. This is why it is untimely and unfitting. In brief, this is why it is unnatural, threatening and inappropriate. This is why it involves discontinuity. And this is why death casts its shadow *back* upon life.

From the standpoint of the Old Testament then, death is understood as God's *judgement* upon man. Yet it is viewed even more as an event in which God and man *are alienated* from one another. And it is this deadly alienation of God and man which constitutes the real misery of death.

(*e*) *Death as alien to God.* Unlike the swan returning to the God Apollo to which the dying Socrates compared himself, man in the Old Testament does not sing hymns of praise to God at the

approach of death. The person who is dying does not return
home to God; he returns to the dust from which he was
created. In this sense, death marks the end of a man's
relationship to God. To put it bluntly: 'The dead do not praise
the Lord' (Ps. 115: 17); and again: 'For Sheol cannot thank
thee, death cannot praise thee; those who go down to the pit
cannot hope for thy faithfulness. The living, the living, he thanks
thee, as I do this day' (Isa. 38: 18f.). For the living, life and
death stand face to face like good and evil (Deut. 30: 15), like
a blessing and a curse (v. 19). This is why the living are
summoned to choose life rather than death (ibid.). Thus in
contrast to Cicero we might say: 'tota fidelium vita est
abrogatio mortis'. The believer's entire life is a renunciation of
death not because he denies but precisely because he affirms the
fact that in every human life death has its hour, and that every
human life has its last hour. Thus integral to the faith of
Israel is the *affirmation of man's finitude*. Faith is thus led to place
not only a high value but the highest possible value upon life
as a denial of death. The exceptionally high value which the
Old Testament gives to life as a denial of death (in the face of
death!) reveals a very clear theological understanding of the
anthropological phenomenon of death. We must begin from the
standpoint of life. To value life as the highest good is a judgement which has its source in faith in Jahweh as the fountain
and fulness of life. Man lives, because and to the extent that
God stands in relation to him. It is incumbent upon man,
therefore, to live his life in a way which is appropriate to that
relationship in which God stands to him. By thus relating
himself and his life to the One who already stands in
relation to him, man makes a distinction between himself and
God. In the Old Testament therefore, 'life' means *to have* a
relationship. Above all, it means to have a relationship to God,
a relationship of salutary distance which is the basis of
appropriate conduct. In the Old Testament, man's life is
determined by his relationships. These relationships are clearly
formulated. They are laid down in the Law: relationships to

one's neighbour, to the nation, to oneself and to God. Men may
seek to obscure and dissolve the simplicity of these relationships.
The attempt to do so, to destroy these life-relationships, is what
the Old Testament calls *sin*. Sin is rebellion against the God
who is related to man in all man's relationships with other
men. Sin exerts a pressure which issues in the absence of
relationships. It renders man relationless. Death thus becomes
one facet of this pressure which drives towards relationlessness.
From the anthropological point of view then, death to this
extent is not merely and not primarily an event at life's end.
It is constantly present as an active possibility in this driving
pressure toward relationlessness.

Sin, then, is the godless pressure which effects relationlessness.
With this pressure, according to the Old Testament, death's
role is extended. It does not merely bring life to a sudden end.
It throws man's conduct into painful disorder by disturbing the
relationships in which he lives. The book of Job is one of the
best examples of this. Death extends its alien power to trespass
upon the orderliness of creation and the good life within it, to
disturb good order and right conduct. When death has actually
occurred, then man's life has become completely relationless.
The dead person is then forever alienated from his God. And
apart from God, everything becomes relationless.

To have died means not only that a man no longer has any
relationship to everything apart from himself. First and foremost, he no longer has any relationship to himself: 'For the
living know (at least) that they will die, but the dead know
nothing' (Eccl. 9: 5). The worst that can be said of the dead
is that their relationship to God has come to an end. In his
final despair, Job plays off death as the power which
alienates from God against God Himself by reminding his
Creator that even for him there may be a time when it will be
too late: 'For now I shall lie in the earth; thou wilt seek me,
but I shall not be' (Job 7: 21). This means that if God is to
help, then he must do it now before death comes and before
its presence is final. For death casts its alien shadow upon

every sphere of life so that in weakness, in sickness, in captivity and when endangered by the enemy, it may alienate life from God and life from life.

As alien to God, death is aggressive. This is not to be understood mythologically. It is to be interpreted in a thoroughly anthropological way. In the midst of life man is threatened by death, and this implies that man poses a threat to himself. Death could be the fulfilment of the relationships in which man's life is lived. This would be the *natural death* which man not only must die but could die. Nevertheless, the Bible speaks of death not so much in terms of what it could be, but chiefly in terms of what it is. It destroys the relationships and breaks the bonds within which alone life can find its fulfilment. In this sense it is essentially active as a negation. It repudiates life by hopelessly alienating man and God from one another. Death is the hopeless case.

(*f*) *Resurrection of the dead?* It is only on the periphery of the Old Testament that the idea arises that there is hope for the dead. As we have seen, talk of deliverance from death which we find mainly in the Psalms refers to the help which is called for in special need, to those occasions when death's role is extended beyond that of bringing life to a sudden end, and to those cases in which the presence of death is felt to be very real. This is why the person whose life has been in danger and who has received deliverance can say, in no sense metaphorically, that he has been delivered from Sheol, from death. Of course in Ps. 139: 8 and in Amos 9: 2 it is expressly asserted that God can intervene in the realm of the dead. But neither of these texts refers to a resurrection from the dead. Only later were such texts (along with Ps. 73 and Job 19) read in the light of a resurrection hope. The same possibly applies with regard to Isa. 26: 19, while it is certainly applicable in the case of Dan. 12: 1. Isa. 26: 14 follows the classical conception of ancient Israel: 'They are dead, they will not live; they are shades, they will not arise.' Nevertheless, only five verses later we read

(Isa. 26: 19): 'Thy dead shall live, their bodies shall rise. O Dwellers in the dust, awake and sing for joy!' Either this statement is intended as a correction of the previous one or it may be that the earlier verse may apply only to the godless. With regard to v. 19 this would suggest that resurrection is promised only to the elect. On the other hand it may be that v. 19 is an illustration which refers to the deliverance of the whole of Israel in her affliction, just as this is most certainly the case in the great vision of the resurrection of the dry bones in Ezek. 37. The decision must remain open.

By contrast with this, Dan. 12: 2 clearly prophesies a resurrection of the dead (within the context of the establishment of the kingdom of God of the end-time): 'And many of those who sleep in the dust of the earth shall awake, some to ever-lasting life, and some to shame and everlasting contempt.' But with regard to Dan. 12 there is certainly no suggestion of a resurrection (from the dead) of *all* those who have died. The contrast: 'to everlasting life—to everlasting contempt' shows that those who are here undergoing the difficult test of suffering will receive the compensation of an eternal reward. The hope of resurrection which is disclosed here is not free from the malicious pleasure which some people take in the misfortune of others.

The statement of the Isianic apocalypse (which is most likely a later addition) seems to fall completely outside the Old Testament framework: 'He will swallow up death for ever' (Isa. 25: 8). However, this prophecy is truly the final consequence of a faith which knows God not only as Creator, but as Lord and as a Partner whose active concern is that the covenant relationship should be governed by *love*. 'For love is strong as death' (Song of Solomon, 8: 6).

New Testament attitudes to death
That attitude to death which is to be found only on the fringes of the Old Testament comes fully into the open in the New Testament: hope in the resurrection of the dead. It is

grounded in the certainty of God's victory over death. To this must be added the fact that this was a victory for which God had to fight. The outcome was not something which was certain from all eternity. It was no foregone conclusion, no runaway victory 'rendering silent every doubt and struggle in victory's higher certainty' and so excluding 'every witness to human need.' In the language of the New Testament, God and death are the opponents. They are enemies. The struggle in which God deals with death, and in which death also has to deal with God is the history which faith tells about Jesus Christ. Accordingly, New Testament attitudes to death are wholly determined by the attitude which is adopted to the history of Jesus Christ. And according to the view expressed in the New Testament, what death is all about is something which is decided by the death of Jesus Christ. In turn, what was decided in the death of Jesus Christ is disclosed in the resurrection of Jesus Christ from the dead.

No doubt, in modern theology (so-called), there are serious debates about the meaning of the death of Jesus and about the 'reality' of his resurrection. The debate is to some extent distorted by that fact that on one side it is insisted that the resurrection is a 'reality'. Further, it is argued that this claim must be immune to any serious criticism. On the other hand there are those who would prefer to ignore the basic fact that the New Testament texts owe their existence in the first place to faith in the resurrection of Jesus Christ from the dead. They would prefer to see the New Testament texts relieved of the burden of just this event. Both of these positions miss the real point of what the dispute is all about. For such categories as 'the real' and 'reality' are totally inappropriate when applied to the resurrection of Jesus. As applied to this event which transcends all other events they can be used only in inverted commas. This is something which genuine piety has always known. Genuine faith has always admitted that all talk of the resurrection runs into logical difficulties. On the other hand, frequent attempts to suggest that talk of the resurrection is to be understood as a more or less arbitrary and optional way of speaking upon which Christian faith is not ultimately dependent, cannot ultimately escape the objection that such a position involves a basically unscientific reading of the New Testament. If these texts have any factual origin at all then it is the Easter-faith. If they are still to be taken seriously in this important theological discussion about the death and resurrection of Jesus Christ then we must call for yet more piety from the over-pious and yet more criticism from the over-critical. But this is by way of a parenthesis!

We cannot deal here with all the different problems which surround the question of the resurrection of Jesus from the dead. The reader is referred to another book in this series where information about these problems can be found.[13] Its results can for our own purposes be presupposed, although some of its judgements differ from my own. In what follows we shall discuss Jesus' death and resurrection in so far as they are relevant to the theological question of man's death. In this connection it will be assumed that the New Testament statements on this question are statements of faith. Dogmatic reflection itself does not forsake the horizon of faith. It reflectively penetrates that horizon. And it is precisely for this reason that it finds itself continually confronted with unfaith.

(a) *Some logical and theological problems in connection with the New Testament view of death.* The contrast between Old Testament and New Testament attitudes to death perhaps becomes most obvious in terms of the linguistic shift which characterises Phil. 1 : 20f.; John 5 : 24; and John 11 : 25f. As far as this problem is concerned, these are the most important texts. There can be no doubt that they are all stamped by the theology of their respective authors. The Pauline text is also influenced by the personal situation of the apostle. Nevertheless, as far as the New Testament attitude to death is concerned, these texts express judgements about the relationship between the life and death (of the Christian) which go right to the heart of the matter.

Paul writes from prison under threat of martyrdom. He rejoices that Christ is preached. He is certain that Christ will be honoured in him 'whether by life or by death. For to me to live is Christ, and to die is gain' (Phil. 1: 20f.). Paul goes on to say that he does not know what to choose: 'life in the flesh', or 'to depart and be with Christ'. Death is by far the best. However, to 'remain in the flesh' is more necessary for the sake of the community.

In contrast to the Old Testament, the striking thing here is the way in which life and death are made to appear relative. Christ can be glorified 'whether by life or by death'. Isaiah had something very different to say: 'For Sheol cannot thank thee, death cannot praise thee, those who go down to the pit cannot hope for thy faithfulness. The living, the living, he thanks thee, as I do this day' (Isa. 38: 18f.). But because of what Christ means to him, Paul thinks differently. Through Christ, life and death are placed in a new relationship to one another. It is significant that in Paul's judgement it is not that Christ belongs together with life and not with death. It is rather that both life *and* death are defined by Jesus Christ. With this correspond some other Pauline texts such as Rom. 14: 8f., and Rom. 8: 38f. These mean that in life as in death we are under the lordship of Jesus Christ so that neither death nor life (nor any other power) can separate us from the love of God which is present in Jesus Christ. Life and death are therefore no longer the criteria which define man's relationship to God. Jesus Christ and faith in him is the one criterion for defining that relationship.

In view of these statements one might well gain the impression that now that life and death are seen to be relative, it will ultimately be a matter of indifference whether one lives or not. This was also the opinion of the Stoic philosophers who could approve suicide as 'a reasonable death'. In view of the need to preserve and guard the freedom of the philosopher, death could be preferred above life. This also amounts to the relativisation of life and death in favour of the higher value of freedom.

For Paul, however, life and death do not possess the same value. Death is not to be valued nore highly than life. If it should seem that death is more welcome to him than life, then the reason for this is that in dying he is not delivered up to the power of death, but to the power of the One who lives and who has conquered death. 'For to this end Christ died and lived again, that he might be Lord both of the dead and of the living' (Rom. 14: 9). Correspondingly, Rom. 6: 9: 'For we know that Christ being raised from the dead will never die again; death no longer has dominion over him.' This becomes the basis for faith's certainty that those who have been baptised will live with Christ (v. 8). Quite remarkably, it can now be said of those who are baptised that they have already died, that they have died with Christ. Therefore although his death is yet before him, the believer can already see his death in retrospect. And because he can already look back upon his death, the believer realises that his present life is in no sense any more his own. It is rather that; 'it is no longer I who live, but Christ who lives in me' (Gal. 2: 20).

How are we to understand this? The confusing language which the apostle seems to be using appears on the one hand to balance and equate life and death as far as the Christian is concerned. This is an equation which the Old Testament definition of the relationship between life and death clearly contradicts. On the other hand, and in similar language, life is clearly given precedence over death, although of course in this case the predicate 'life' is to be understood in relation to the subject to whom it belongs, namely, Jesus Christ risen from the dead. This life which belongs to Jesus Christ is obviously different from the life possessed by all other men. The life which every other man has is a life which *leads to death*, whereas the life possessed by Jesus Christ is a life which *emerges from death*. To the extent that Jesus Christ *shares* his life with those who wish to belong to him, they also are set free from death even though they must yet die. However, the death which still awaits them is now so different from the death to which man's life leads that it no longer constitutes a challenge to life. The most pointed expression of this is to be found in the Gospel according to St. John: 'I am the resurrection and the life. He who believes in me though he die, yet shall he live, and whoever lives and believes in me shall never die' (John 11 : 25f.). And again in the direct language of the Fourth Gospel: 'He who hears my word and believes him who sent me, has eternal life; he does not come into judgement, but has passed from death to life' (John 5 : 24).

It is almost impossible for language to express all this without becoming ambiguous and confusing. The language of the first Christian communities and of their 'theologians' as it were, explodes. After centuries of philosophical work dedicated to finding words appropriate to things and to bringing them into a proper relationship with each other so that there might be a measure of order on the realms of being and thought, the Christian faith is now responsible for causing an immense disturbance in the sphere of language. It reaches the very limits of incomprehensibility, even to such an extent that the apostle is compelled to remind the congregation in Corinth that God is a God of peace and not of confusion (1 Cor. 14: 33). The incomprehensible will only become comprehensible when we recall what it is that is fighting for expression. It is then that this incredible disturbance of the language of faith becomes the fruitful stimulus for a new ordering of thought which dares to think the unthinkable notion (which at best is said to be acceptable only 'in the last analysis' or 'at the end of all things'), that the resurrection from the dead has already taken place. Put to death on a cross, Jesus lives. This explosion of language brings to expression a new being. It can find expression in no other way than by letting the linguistic tradition so to say, burst its banks.

The world is at work in our language. It is through language also that we deal with the world. Faith also speaks the world's language. But it cannot speak this language without changing it. For at work in the language of faith is the event of the resurrection of Jesus from the dead. It is this event which prevents language from becoming irretrievably embedded in tradition in such a way that it remains bound to ancient forms. Faith deals with the world according to the way in which it uses language. In turn, the language of the world in which faith's concern is active is changed. With regard both to being and language things never remain as they were. This can be seen most clearly in the attempt to speak of the resurrection of Jesus Christ itself. In this endeavour one must be prepared to let the traditional language about life and death 'explode'.

In order to avoid any misunderstanding it should be pointed out that here we are not referring to the use of the term 'resurrection of the dead'. It is quite clear that before the emergence of the Christian communities the expectation of a resurrection of the dead already existed. Jewish apocalyptic already possessed a store of expressions and ideas to represent this notion. Christian faith made use of this. But it did so only because of its belief in an event which had already happened, the resurrection of Jesus Christ from the dead. This meant that all previous history and every succeeding event on earth and between heaven and earth was evaluated in a completely new way. If Jesus was raised from the dead then the end of time was present in the midst of time; in the very midst of its course judgement had been passed upon the world. The further course of the world, the history and time remaining had to be judged anew. It was now impossible to regard it as a process begun and laid down in the ancient past now running out toward its end. It was now impossible to see it as determined by fate and ending in bankruptcy. Christian faith understood the world against the horizon of a new history beginning with the resurrection of Jesus Christ, a new history with a correspondingly new understanding of time (E. Fuchs).[14] And it was this new understanding of time which effected the explosion of language in terms of which the relationship between life and death was defined anew.

If any attempt should be made to steer this linguistic unrest of the New Testament with regard to this question in the direction of some terminological clarity (and this unrest must be clearly distinguished from mere excitement), then one must also take into consideration the fact that the disturbance which characterises this new talk of death is not something which can be suppressed with the help of terminological precision. The endeavour to arrive at terminological precision should rather be a means by which this unrest which is present in the New Testament attitude to death may be more properly identified. In this regard, the search for terminological exactitude and the information to be derived from it should lead to debate and not to silence.

Paul's remarks about the Christian's attitude to death require that certain distinctions be made between the different nuances of meaning of those expressions which belong to the word-family surrounding the word 'death'. Like John, Paul can say that the believer has already died, that through the law he has died to the law (Gal. 2: 19), that he has been buried with Christ in baptism (Rom. 6: 4). On the other hand, Paul can also say that the death which is still before him he can count as gain (Phil. 1: 21). And lastly, he can also say that he carries the death of Jesus in the body (2 Cor. 4: 10).

It is clear that Paul understands the death which the believer *has already died* as death in the *negative* sense. It is this death which is to be feared. It is this death which is the result of sin (Rom. 6: 23), the consequence of that pressure exerted toward relationlessness which corresponds to the break in man's relationship with God. As the consequence of alienation from God it is also the expression of the truth about this alienation. This death reveals what happens when man merely seeks to realise himself in all that he does and in all that he refuses to do: he loses his life and forfeits the right to live.

So understood, death is thus not the result of some special act of God due to the nature of man's sin. Nor is it an arbitrary divine interference in the sense that on account of the nature of sin itself God must punish the sinner. It is rather the case that this is an event demanded by the very nature of sin itself. To this extent it constitutes a punishment. 'Death is guilt made visible' (Rahner).[15] Thus it is wholly appropriate to say that the sinner forfeits his life and the right to live.

The notion of a forfeiture is particularly fitting here. For when man incurs this death he himself is at the same time striving to achieve it. The godless pressure toward relationlessness takes concrete shape in man's actual conduct. Man's attempt to destroy his relationship to God happens not outside or apart from this relationship but within it in that man maintains the relationship in such a way that God himself becomes superfluous. This is what Paul calls self-justification. God is reduced to the level of one who is required to confirm man's estimate of himself. Man judges and God should approve. Man pronounces himself justified and free and it is God's job to add his seal. With this there goes the recognition that God should certainly be above all things, enthroned above man on high. But God should be above man only so that under him man may have a free hand to be his own judge. In setting God above man in such a way God is degraded and disparaged. And this is how man destroys his relationship to God. In comparison with this, modern atheism is a relatively harmless phenomenon.

Thus man forfeits his life and his God-given right to life. According to the New Testament this is the nature of the death which the sinner must die. In terms of the tradition this is the *curse of death*. It is the curse of the evil action which throws everything into relationlessness, which continues to bring forth evil until it finally incurs that death upon itself which reveals the nothingness and emptiness of the relationless life by bringing it to naught. The New Testament speaks of this death as a curse as though it were some kind of power. It rules (Rom. 5: 14, 17). Man is delivered up to its power. But this annihilating power of death is the power which man himself chooses to take on as his opponent. On earth there is nothing more powerful than the unintended consequences of our action. The curse of death reigns over the consequences of our actions. It is man himself who is responsible for this. To this extent we can therefore say that the event of the curse of death is man's own deed. This is the death which man brings upon himself.

When Paul speaks of the curse of death and says that the Christian no longer has it before him (although another end still awaits him), he gives expression to the fact that the end of man's life may be viewed from quite a different perspective than that of sin. Death does not have to be the death which is a curse. Dying may also be an end which need hold no terrors. It can even be a gain. How is this to be understood?

It is clear that this is to be understood in the sense that the believer is exempt from the curse of death, the death which man brings upon himself. This is what he means when he says, 'I have died.' The dead are not in the habit of speaking. Nevertheless, when Paul says, 'through the law I have died to the law', then this can only mean that he is no longer under the sway of the curse of death. According to what we have just said, this means that man is set free from the consequences of his own drive toward relationlessness. The power which man summons up against himself so that he can no longer escape the consequences of his own actions is broken. The question of the 'wretched' I, that which causes man to forfeit his life ('Who will deliver me from this body of death?' Rom. 7: 24), is now one which can be answered. We shall return to this in due course.

Before taking up this question, in this chapter we must still try to give more precision to the notion that man's death can be free from the curse of death. If death as a curse is the consequence of man's drive toward relationlessness, then any deliverance from this death must consist in the creation of a new foundation for those relationships in which alone human life can find its fulfilment. We must note carefully however, that this is not the question of those relationships which make human life possible. It is a question of the 'condition humaine'. To produce

new relationships of this kind is a *creative* act; it is *the* creative
act, the work of God the Creator. These new relationships are
thus founded upon a new relationship between God and man
in which *man* is created anew (2 Cor. 5: 17). If the initial
creation prepares the way for man, the necessary relationships
for life to be lived existing before man's creation, then the new
creation is to be understood as being effected from the opposite
direction. It begins with the new man, so that with him and
through him, the new relationships demanded by the 'condition humaine' may be created.

The essential thing about these relationships is that they
cannot be broken. As the end of man's life, death therefore does
not involve an abrupt break with life. God's creative relationship to man excludes the possibility that this relationship can
be broken, but it does not exclude the fact that human life
comes to its end. With the idea of the Creator we usually
combine the notion of the beginning, of the beginning of the
creation. But is this justified? With regard to creation and the
biblical notion of the Creator, *both* beginning *and* end are
involved. Theologically speaking, an end is to be distinguished
from a breaking-off in the sense that as far as the latter is
concerned, nothing follows. Beyond this hiatus there is nothing,
only the total absence of relation. Whereas on the other side of
the end there is God. Beyond that which has come to an
end there is not simply nothing, but the same God who was in
the beginning. This is something which we have to learn and
try to understand: it is not only the beginning which
constitutes a blessing; the end is also an act of grace.

This end is *God's* act. It is not the end of man's own
making. The end which man prepares for himself and for other
men is the death which he must suffer as a curse. Even to be
compelled to die, to accept one's death and thus be enabled to
die, is to die the death which is a curse. It is for this reason
that we should not seek martyrdom.

The end of life which is not of man's making is of course
also an event which man must endure and suffer. In suffering

this death man is passive. He is passive too, but in a different way, when he endures the curse of death which he has brought upon himself as a consequence of his own actions. When he undergoes the curse of death, man is subject to an activity which he must endure with suffering. On the other hand, the end of life which is released from that curse is endured with a passiveness conditioned and tempered by the activity of the Creator. Passive endurance cannot be an evil. And here we may learn also that not everything we have to endure must necessarily be painful.

There is thus a passiveness which belongs to man's nature. Without it he would not be man. It involves the fact that one is born, that one is loved, that one dies. It would be mistaken to conclude therefore that because man is born of man and loved by men, the basically passive attitude of human existence which this implies is what it is apart from any divine activity. God is the Creator of all men. And whenever a man is truly loved, God is not far. He is most near to the man who truly loves his fellow men. What man does, then, does not exclude what God the Creator does.

But the activity of God in *bringing to an end* does exclude human participation. In this process any human action must be regarded as an illegitimate encroachment upon the action of God. Later we shall have occasion to deal with the ethical problems which this point involves. For the moment, our concern is a theological one. And as far as this question is concerned, the decisive thing is that in death, understood as the end of human life as willed by God, man is brought to a final passiveness. This is a passiveness which is integral to his humanity. It sets a salutary limit to his life.

It will be appropriate at this point to indicate our disagreement with a theory taken up in philosophy and one which is impressively put forward in Catholic theology. It is the theory that death is the final decision, the act which consummates human life (Rahner);[16] 'the one act of the will' (Boros).[17] From a biblical point of view, this interpretation is untenable. It is not even valid for death understood as a curse, the death of the sinner, because the death of the one whose action leads to the forfeiture of his life is not a death which he wills.

Set free from the curse of death, life's end may therefore be understood more precisely as man's *natural death*, as the end of that existence which he is by nature. It is not because of his nature but because of his guilt as a sinner that this natural death can become a curse. From the quite remarkable terminological fact that the New Testament makes a temporal distinction between the curse of death which threatens man's existence and the true end of man's life we can see that the end of man's life does not have to be a curse: both Paul and John can say of believers that this death prior to life's ending is something which for them is already past. In the Book of Revelation quite the opposite is said to apply as far as the godless are concerned, namely, that after life's ending this death will still await them in a final judgement (Rev. 20: 11–15). Definitively understood as an annihilation, this death is called the 'second death' (Rev. 20: 6, 14).[18]

This talk of a *second death*, to which we can find reference in the history of religions, in the literature of ancient Egypt and in the Mandaean texts, is misleading. It conceals the logical difficulties which the New Testament attitudes to death imply. And it was an unfortunate decision when the church tradition, chiefly under the powerful influence of Augustine, took up this linguistic usage. That this adoption of apocalyptic language was found to be acceptable can be explained by the fact that talk of a second death was particularly suitable for preparing the way for the entrance into Christian theology of the Platonic understanding of death. Augustine developed a very differentiated doctrine of death in which he attempted to unite the biblical and Platonic views. In theory, four kinds of death are to be distinguished: the death of the soul, which is nevertheless regarded as immortal, the death of the body, the death of both body and soul

understood as the death of the whole man, and the—second—
death of the whole man, the man who is resurrected from the
dead and who exists once more in the unity of body and
soul. According to Augustine, the death of the soul occurs
when God leaves the soul; the death of the body when the
soul, as the life-principle of the body, leaves the body. However,
the death of the whole man occurs when the soul which has
been forsaken by God leaves the body. And the second
death occurs when the soul which God has forsaken is reunited
with its soul-forsaken body. Thus raised from the dead man
lives only to suffer *eternal death* and to endure endless
suffering.

This understanding of the second death as eternal death
is the exact opposite of the Platonic understanding of death.
(The Platonic conception had been taken over and corresponded
to the notion of the 'first death'). Nevertheless, what
Augustine has to say about the second death comes very
close to what the Platonic Socrates hints at in one of the
myths of the 'Phaedo' concerning the souls of incorrigible
criminals (107c): for those who do not will the good,
immortality (precisely for them!) is a great danger, for there
is always the possibility that the wicked will forever remain
in Hades.[19] In keeping with this Augustine says that it is not
the death which 'occurs at the soul's release from the body',
but the death which occurs 'through the joining of both to
eternal torment' that is 'of all evils the greatest.' For 'it can
never go so ill with man in death as when death itself will not
die.'[20]

This and similar attempts to give some dogmatic content
to the apocalyptic reference to the second death is theologically
and hermeneutically questionable. The problem is that any
connection with death as that event which marks the end of
human life, logically and theologically speaking, is as good as
ignored. However, it is impossible to say this of the Johannine
and Pauline statements concerning the death which the
believer already has behind him. From a logical point of view

it is quite legitimate to use the word 'death' (which always denotes the end of earthly life), in some negatively qualified sense. For example, we speak of the fear of death, using the word with this negative qualification. This enables us to make a distinction between the negatively qualified use of the word 'death' and its function as denoting the fact of life's end. This is why we have made a distinction between the curse of death and natural death. However, apart from the meaning of the word 'death' as 'the end of human life', this other, qualified, negative meaning of the word would have no function. The qualified, negative use always requires the presupposition that the word 'death' means 'the end of life'. Death understood as a curse is the end of life. It is an end which is terrifying and which involves rupture and separation. This also applies with regard to those statements which imply that this death understood as a curse has already occurred. Quite consistently Paul concludes that one must therefore regard oneself as *dead* (Gal. 2: 19; Rom. 6: 11); that he who has thus died no longer lives and no longer lives of himself (2 Cor. 5: 15; Rom. 6: 10). 'I live, but yet not I, Christ lives in me.' It is quite logical to talk of death as a curse. The assertion that the believer no longer has this death before him is a theological assertion which certainly calls for proof. Nevertheless, from a logical point of view, such a thesis is entirely defensible.

Any reference to a second death beyond this life and beyond life's end can hardly be logically justified. Of course in terms of numbers it involves some reference to the first death understood as life's end. But with regard to content the meaning of the word 'death' is here driven to the point of absurdity. The first death is merely a numerical presupposition. Talk of the second death does not therefore permit any serious consideration of the first death understood as the end of life.

Chapter Five

The Death of Jesus Christ

(Death as God's Passion)

The death of Jesus as the event of salvation
To ask about death is to enquire about life. In enquiring about death, theology questions the life which is indebted to the death of Jesus Christ. To what extent does the death of Jesus Christ determine the life of the Christian? And of what significance is the death of Jesus Christ for the death which we all must die?

It is due to the significance of the death of Jesus for the formation of the Christian faith that we can enquire about *the Christian understanding of death* at all. The proclamation of the death of this one man has a function in the history of our world which nothing else can displace. It would be no exaggeration to say that apart from the death of Jesus there would have been no Christian proclamation, no Christian hope or trust in God, and no genuinely Christian understanding of the word 'God' itself. The death of Jesus is of decisive significance for the believer's attitude to life. Thus it is also of decisive importance for his attitude to death. For Paul in particular, although not only for him, the death of Jesus was the one event of salvation.

It is impossible for us to discover what significance *Jesus himself* attached to his death. Exegetical investigation of the New Testament has demonstrated that it is most probable that all the New Testament statements referring to the death of Jesus as the salvation event arose only after the event of his death. They presuppose the event of the resurrection, or, more precisely, they presuppose faith in the Resurrected One. A man who unconditionally announced God's nearness

to the godless, who uncompromisingly set forth the law of
love with the demand to love the loveless, was bound to
evoke a bitter response both in word and action (and not
merely from the ruling authorities), and must to some extent
have reckoned with the possibility that his life might end
violently. However, to judge by the sayings which have come
down to us and which in all probability originated with
Jesus himself, he did not declare that the end of his own
life would be of significance for the life and death of other
men. Nor do we know how he accepted the sentence of
death which was passed upon him. It is quite likely also
that the words of the Crucified One were only later attributed
to the dying Jesus. However, the tradition that Jesus cried
out when he died is quite firmly established.

There can also be no doubt that at first Jesus' disciples
experienced his crucifixion as quite the opposite of a saving
event. 'They all left him and fled' (Mark 14: 50; cf. Luke 24:
21; John 20: 19). It required the specific experience that
God had not forsaken this man who had been executed as a
criminal, and that it was God who after his execution had
brought certain people to the realisation that Jesus was the
representative of a new, future life, before any positive
significance could be attached to the death of Jesus. It also
required time for this experience to mature. It did not happen
by itself nor was it universally experienced. Paul, whose
letters are the oldest documents in the New Testament, could
of course refer to traditions in which Jesus' death was
variously interpreted as the salvation event, for instance, as
propitiatory atonement (1 Cor. 11: 24; 15: 3), as a paschal
offering (1 Cor. 5: 7), or as the renewal of the covenant
(Rom. 3: 24f.). Yet at the same time there were communities
in which Jesus' resurrection was understood in such a way
that his death appeared to be wholly insignificant.

Of course, the apostle *Paul* regarded this as a complete
misunderstanding and as the one total misapprehension which
was sufficient to put the validity of Christian faith itself in

question. As far as Paul is concerned the case is quite the opposite. The resurrection of Jesus is a demonstration of the eternal significance of the cross and the death of Jesus. This is why the apostle proclaims the risen Christ as the One crucified for us. This is something very different from the mere assumption that the crucified One is no longer dead, that he is alive. If it were simply a matter of proclaiming the resurrection of Jesus as the event which somehow annuls his death then it is most unlikely that the 'Gospel' as a literary genre would ever have arisen. Based on the event of the resurrection, the oldest Gospel, that of Mark, is simply 'the story of the passion with an extended introduction' (Kähler).[1] Because of the resurrection it is now made clear why God's 'beloved Son' (Mark 1: 11) had to die. The story of Jesus must be told as a history which must necessarily end in death. According to God's will this life ought to end in death (Mark 8: 31). The New Testament has very little to say about the new life of the resurrected One, the Christ who has been exalted to God's right hand. However, it has a great deal to say about the earthly Jesus, about that which can only be understood in the light of the resurrection. This applies above all to Jesus' death.

It is obvious that the New Testament offers differing *interpretations* of the death of Jesus. There are contrasts and differences here which require critical evaluation.

Pauline theology as a whole is a theology of the cross and nothing else. By contrast, in the Acts of the Apostles, the death of Jesus is almost always regarded as a foil to the resurrection, and as a judicial error which God in turn has set right. Again, in the Letter to the Hebrews, Jesus' death is understood as the requirement which renders him eligible for the office of heavenly High Priest. At the same time it is understood as the breakthrough which brings freedom from a world which is given over to death and the fear of death. When Jesus' life was interpreted in the light of the event of the incarnation of the divine Son or the Word, his death received a different meaning. The decisive event of salvation now stood at the beginning of Jesus' historical existence. Correspondingly, his death was understood as the culmination of his obedience and self-surrender. This is already the interpretation which is given in the hymn in Paul's letter to the Philippians (Phil. 2: 6ff., to which certain additions have been made by way of correction), and of course in the Gospel of John. Here, the death of Jesus is seen as the victory of the 'light of life' over the darkness which could not overcome it.

These are merely some examples to demonstrate that the New Testament offers us no single, uniform doctrine of the death of Jesus. Nevertheless, this varied and even contradictory witness does not render a dogmatic consideration of the meaning of the death of Jesus impossible. We must only be clear about that fact that the Bible is not a book which supplies unproblematic answers. It is a book which speaks to us in our need. It poses questions and presents problems which compel thought. The person who reads the Bible with understanding, with the sincere wish that it should speak to him, cannot avoid assuming responsibility for the Word *on his own account.* This is really why the Bible is there. Normally, we can appeal to theology and the church as the requisite supports in this connection. However, to assume responsibility for the Word on one's own account necessarily means finding words to express the things of faith with which others can concur without thereby being themselves dispensed from taking on responsibility on their own part for what it is that these words have to say.

The matter with which we are concerned is the death of Jesus Christ. Being responsible to and for the Word with regard to the biblical texts means that we cannot set aside the general theological investigation of the problem of death. In this chapter we shall discuss the question of that necessity which made the death of Jesus decisive for the origin of Christian faith. Having done this we shall then consider the significance of the death of Jesus for the question of our own death.

The life of Jesus and faith in God
In the brief period of his public ministry, Jesus proclaimed
God's unconditional, saving presence both to those who wished
to listen and to those who did not. He did this both in
word and action.

Jesus *spoke* of the kingdom of God, or, as it may be better
translated, of the rule of God. And he spoke of this rule of God
in such a way that its nearness was experienced not as the
assault of a power-hungry oppressor, but as the liberating
immediacy of a God concerned with man. Jesus himself
pointed out that man's concern should be his fellow man.
Only in this way can God's concern for man become an
event, when man is concerned with his fellow men.

It will be appropriate at this point to insert an incidental
note concerning another alternative position with regard to this
matter. Generally it has found wide acceptance but is quite
inadequate. The questionable alternative is this: either divinity
or humanity. This is the alternative which confronts us even in
the work of such a clear-thinking exegete as Herbert Braun.
To suggest that it is not from 'directly from above' that God
'approaches and encounters man in his misery and guilt here
on earth'[2] is to introduce an extremely abrupt alternative.
The notion of 'above' is of course a metaphor which can
easily be misapplied. And this is something which Christianity
could have learned from Martin Luther and not just from
Ernst Bloch who can clearly associate God only with the
notion of oppressive authority. The important thing is not
whether one says 'from above' or 'from ahead' or 'out of the
future' or 'from alongside' when one is speaking of the action
of God. What is decisive when speaking of God's action is that
one says 'of God' or 'from God'. God's action has its source
in God himself. This was what 'directly from above' once
used to mean. That God's action encounters us in and through
other people does not in any way exclude the fact that although
in this sense it is indirect, the action still has its source in
God. To introduce an abrupt alternative here is to break off

the work of theology precisely at that point where its real difficulties and subtleties are just beginning to appear. But for the moment, enough has been said about this.

Jesus preached not only with words. By his *actions* he also demonstrated the nearness of the rule of God who was concerned with man. In his conduct, Jesus gave himself to other men, particularly to those who were refused recognition and acceptance by those of their fellow men who had allowed their lives to become circumscribed by regulations. In surrendering himself as a man to men Jesus demonstrated the nearness of God. Jesus' conduct no less than his preaching was a *parable* of God's nearness.

The purpose of any parable is to make one single point. We laugh when someone has told a successful joke. In our laughter what has been said 'comes home' to us. At the same time the hearer finds himself 'at home' with what has been said. Every successful joke thus draws the hearer out of himself. In the same way, at the conclusion of any of Jesus' parables there comes the point of the parable. The hearer is grasped by what has been spoken and in turn he himself also grasps the point of the parable. Now one may either consent to accept and stand by the point made, or begin to resist the implications of what one has let oneself in for simply by listening to the parable. Now if Jesus' conduct is also a parable of God's nearness, then it must also provoke acceptance or opposition. Because of his attempt to announce and to illustrate God's nearness to publicans and sinners by sharing in their table-fellowship Jesus was accused of being a glutton and a winebibber (Matt. 11 : 19). Such is an example of the bitter opposition which his claim aroused.

The decision which Jesus made possible for his fellow men and which he also called forth from them was made all the more urgent by the fact that Jesus' announcement of God's nearness was bound up with a certain *temporal expectation*. It must be recognised that Jesus understood the nearness of God's rule as drawing near in time, and as almost

immediate in its temporal proximity. This is what is called
'the expectation of the nearness of the end' (Ger.; Naher-
wartung), and it is frequently stressed that with this notion Jesus
fell victim to the generally accepted, contemporary apocalyptic
attitude to the end of all things. Jesus' expectation was in fact
that in a new world he would drink wine on earth with his
disciples (Mark 14: 25). However, there can be no doubt
that it turned out otherwise. Jesus was put to death before
the history of the world had reached its end. Even today
its end has not yet come and it is open to us to ask even whether
it has moved one single step nearer to its end.

It is obviously quite another question whether conversely,
the end, understood in terms of its content as God's nearness
in his concern for man, is not in fact closer to man in his
history than any purely temporal considerations would lead us
to suppose. The phenomena which the apocalyptists expected
would accompany the end of history are ultimately not some
law with which God must comply. It is perfectly clear that
Jesus was also of this opinion. He showed little interest in
'reckoning the times' or in offering descriptions of the cosmic
signs which would mark the end of the world. As far as
he was concerned, God's nearness was much nearer than this,
therefore his preference for giving *temporal* expression to its
proximity had also at the same time to be interpreted in a
personal way. Jesus *believed* in the nearness of God. This was
much more than a hope in something yet to come. To witness
the approach of that which is to come means that it has
ceased to be an object of hope. It is a matter of certainty. We
may even say that Jesus was more certain of the nearness of
God than he was of himself. Without in any way becoming
untrue to his world, he knew himself to be wholly determined
by the rule of God. Governed and determined in a personal
way, the temporal distinction between 'already' and 'not yet'
is overcome though not wholly annulled. It is only in this
sense that we can understand such a text as Luke 11: 20:
'But if it is by the finger of God that I cast out demons, then

the kingdom of God has come upon you.' The view that Jesus
was wrong with regard to his 'expectation of the nearness
of the end' is therefore alike both correct and mistaken.

We may illustrate this with reference to another problem
which involves the notion of being personally determined
by the nearness of God's rule. Jesus claimed no *messianic titles*
for himself and did not present himself as a person to be treated
with distinction. It was the Easter community which gave
him the christological titles, naming him Messiah, Son of God,
Son of Man, Lord and Word of God. The lustre of these
titles give expression to the splendour which surrounded
Jesus' earthly life. The story of this life would be told in the
Christian community. But between his life on earth and the
rise of the Easter community certain things had happened
which caused Jesus to appear in a new light: Easter. Prior to
this Jesus' life was seen in a different way. It could not have
been otherwise. My own view on the matter is that knowing
himself to be wholly and completely determined by God's
rule, Jesus could not make use of any of the messianic
titles without at the same time overplaying the temporal
distinction between its 'presence and its future. For him, all
the messianic titles would at once have been both too much
and too little. Too much, because the kingdom of God
which Jesus announced to everyone as actively imminent, was
not (yet) in actual fact within reach. Too little, because Jesus
knew that his dealings were with *God himself* to such an
extent that even the coming of the Son of Man was bound
up with the decisions which Jesus provoked (Mark 8: 38).

We also might well ask whether all these titles for Jesus
have always said both too much and too little, and perhaps
too little rather than too much. It may be that all these
titles with which people were familiar long before Jesus'
birth were not rather meant to enrich Jesus' human poverty
and humility. Who the true Messiah, Son of Man or Son of
God really is, is something which must be decided with
reference to the person so named. It is no accident that the

title 'Messiah' for Jesus became a name: Jesus Christ.

Nor is it accidental that the need to give distinction to Jesus with titles of honour and to allow one of those titles to form part of his name first arose *after his death*. During his earthly life Jesus had neither demanded nor even expected faith in himself. He made faith in God possible in a new way. He was a *Proclaimer* of the rule of God. He became the *Proclaimed* only after his earthly life had come to an end. Precisely in what way this qualitative turn of events is to be understood is one of the basic problems of modern theology.

Jesus' death and faith in Jesus

Why did the Proclaimer become the Proclaimed? To answer this question we must turn to the Easter faith. Faith in the God who raised Jesus from the dead expresses nothing other than the relationship in which God stood to Jesus of Nazareth in his death. To understand this is the most urgent task which Christian faith still faces. What is of the utmost importance here is nothing less than the true (Christian) meaning of the words 'God' and 'man'. For Christian faith in *God's incarnation* originated with faith in Jesus Christ. The position which I am seeking to defend runs as follows: the faith that God became man did not only arise *after* the death of Jesus; it is grounded *in* the death of Jesus. It was only later that this faith was brought into relationship with the birth of Jesus. The divine attitude which was final and decisive for Jesus himself was the expression of God's relationship to a dead man. This is what the proclamation of the resurrection of Jesus is all about. It communicates that which took place in Jesus' death. However it is not only a communication; it also makes possible our participation. The believer is able to participate in that which took place in Jesus' death.

Accordingly, if we are to understand the death of Jesus, it will depend entirely upon the *perspective toward it* which we adopt: from the standpoint of the life which he lived, or

from the way in which God stood to this life which ended
in death. How Jesus' death is to be understood from the point
of view of the life he lived is a historical question. In any
attempt to answer it faith may prove to be a hindrance
rather than a help. This is because faith already knows Jesus
as the risen One, and when it is a question of evaluating the
life and death of Jesus it has difficulty in abstracting itself
from this knowledge. On the other hand, an examination
of the death of Jesus on the basis of his resurrection is hardly
possible without resorting to the language of faith (in Jesus
Christ!). To understand *today* how the death of Jesus was
originally grasped and expressed in terms of the language of
faith is also a historical question. However, it would be
theologically irresponsible if we were to seek to avoid this
question.

From the point of view of the life he lived we may make
the following historical points about the death of Jesus: Jesus
was put to death by the Roman authorities probably on the
14th or 15th Nisan, circa AD 30. He died an extremely painful
death on a cross, a death which according to Roman legal
practice was normally reserved for slaves and criminals. The
reason for his execution can no longer be determined with any
accuracy. It is possible that Jesus was denounced as a political
agitator. In co-operation with the Roman authorities, his
Jewish opponents must have had reason to take theological
offence because of his preaching and conduct.

That Jesus claimed to be the Messiah and for this reason
was put to death is a claim which first arose within the
Christian community. This can hardly fit with the real
reasons behind his death. More likely is the tradition that one
of the men who had shared his company betrayed him. We
know little or nothing about Jesus' own attitude to his death.
Like many of his Jewish contemporaries he believed in the
resurrection of the dead. However, he did not relate this
notion with his own death or speak of it in connection with
his own death. The prophecies concerning the suffering,

death and resurrection of Jesus have been projected backwards. The 'words from the cross' have also been affected by the way in which the Christian community interpreted his death. One saying which most probably goes back to Jesus himself is the prayer, 'My God, my God, why hast thou forsaken me?' (Mark 15: 34; Matt. 27: 46). The words are from Psalm 22: 2. However, in the knowledge that this same Psalm ends in a triumphant trust in God, these words could also have been put into Jesus' mouth after the event. Jesus cried out when he died. We cannot exclude the possibility that his death was one of utter despair.

If the reasons for Jesus' violent death lay in certain aspects of his preaching and conduct then this becomes a possibility which requires serious consideration. It is a possibility with which he must have reckoned himself. However, we should not imagine that on the cross Jesus died the death of a hero. The self-composure and even serenity with which Socrates met a criminal's death are absent in the case of the historical Jesus. The fact that his followers fled indicates how difficult it was for them to relate what it was that he willed with the fact of his execution. In the 'Phaedo', it is reported by someone who was with Socrates at the time that in his last hour those who were present were affected by a 'curious' mood, 'between laughing and crying' (57c–59e).[3] How unlike Gethsemane: 'My soul is sorrowful unto death' (Mark 14: 34).

The only point of contact for a theology which begins from the *opposite* direction in the attempt to grasp the significance of the death Jesus died is the fact that his work and ministry came to an abrupt and violent end. Because of what had happened to Jesus himself, the nearness of the gracious God in his concern for man which Jesus had proclaimed in word and action now seemed quite absurd. And it may well be that his final cry was a cry of despair at this divine absurdity.

However, shortly after his death, *Jesus himself was proclaimed as the nearness of God*, and as the Son of God. Faith in God, which Jesus had made possible in a new way, now became valid as faith in Jesus Christ. After his death, Jesus was no longer only the witness to faith in God. Like God himself he had become the object of faith. In the attempt to understand the death of Jesus *from the opposite direction*, these are the historically ascertainable facts upon which theological interpretation will be based.

We can observe an important qualitative difference between the attitude of the disciples prior to and after Jesus' death. There can be no dispute about this and it is of decisive importance for this line of interpretation. We can recognise this qualitative difference in terms of language, and also in the titles attributed to Jesus which were intended to give expression to the uniqueness of this man's relationship to God. From among the many it was the title 'Christ' which clearly took precedence. However, the assertion of this unique relationship between Jesus and God carries with it the implication that Jesus is of unique importance for all men. This meant that faith in Jesus as the Christ was a missionary faith which had to be spread beyond every frontier.

If we are to discover the reasons for this qualitative change of circumstances which led to faith in Jesus then we must first of all examine a negative argument which has its basis in the nature of faith itself. It is clearly of the essence of faith that that which is believed is characterised by absence and withdrawal. With reference to Heb. 11: 1 and 2 Cor. 5: 7, Scholasticism expressed this notion with the somewhat problematic statement: 'Objectum fidei est res non visa'—the object of faith is a divine thing which cannot be seen.[4] Under 'withdrawal' here we are to understand a mode of existence in which absence and presence are closely interrelated, as for example, is the case with every kind of hope. However, while hope is determined by that which is not yet present, faith is determined by that which is already present. Now as long as Jesus was in the flesh and present among the living he could certainly call for faith in God, however he could not demand faith in himself. Through his death, however, Jesus was withdrawn from among the living. In this sense then, his death was the negative condition for the possibility that Jesus could become the object of faith.

In this respect, the meaning of Jesus' death as a withdrawal, and the importance of this for faith in Jesus should not be underestimated because here it is precisely the death of Jesus which forms the bridge between the Easter-faith and Jesus' earthly life. As the *withdrawal* and absence of Jesus' Person, death is the means by which the life he lived is *integrated* so as to constitute a unique identity. Through death, the purpose and point of the life he lived is now united and made one with his person as withdrawn and absent. Only in this way can faith in Jesus be understood as a relationship to an irreplaceable Person. We may be enabled to grasp this with the help of a question which at first sight may appear misleading but which nevertheless helps to keep the problem under control. It is simply this: why was it that men believed in Jesus and not in John the Baptist? Why was it that God raised this man from the dead and not the other? (Ebeling).[5]

However, were it not for the fact that after his death there *actually was* such a thing as faith in Jesus all this would amount to no more than idle speculation. This cannot be understood *apart* from the fact that Jesus lived and died, but neither can it be understood *on the basis of* Jesus' life and death alone. That his followers should continue to be his disciples for other reasons and by other means was not to be taken for granted. For as it in fact turned out, rather than continuing in their discipleship, his followers forsook him and fled.

However, it did not end with the flight of the disciples. There arose faith in Jesus. And faith's own explanation for this is that *God* had revealed his glory through the dead Jesus. The nearness of God's rule, that which had determined Jesus' earthly life, that to which he had appealed and cried out in his death, showed itself to be immediately present in the death of Jesus. This was the experience of the Easter-faith, and it was this that men had to experience: in death, the

Proclaimer and the content of his proclamation *have become identical*. The Proclaimer himself has now become the Proclaimed. Thus faith's own ground and presupposition for faith in Jesus is God's *identification* with him in his death.

It is important to understand that faith in Jesus was not something distinct from faith in God. They were not in competition with one another. The question of faith in Jesus concerned nothing less than faith in God itself. Indeed it is with reference to faith in Jesus that the question of faith in God is truly and clearly decided. It was by identifying himself with a dead man that God defined himself to faith first and foremost as the *true* God. It is in this sense that Christian faith in the incarnation, in God becoming man, is grounded in the death of Jesus, or more precisely, in the attitude of God toward Jesus in his death. It is solely in the context of God's conduct toward him in this event that the question of the *necessity* of Jesus' death and its decisiveness for faith in him can appear meaningful.

If God conducted himself toward the dead Jesus by identifying himself with this dead man, then this means that the living God and this dead man are identical—an extremely paradoxical identity indeed! It is this paradoxical identity between the living God and the dead Jesus which brings God himself into contact with death. In this meeting with death God himself did not die. But we should not simply regard it as inevitable or self-evident that God should have used this occasion to reveal himself as the One who calls non-being into being and who imparts new being to that which is no more. Faith in Jesus' resurrection from the dead is hardly something which can simply be taken for granted. And there are good reasons why the only appropriate response to this event is one of gratitude and thanksgiving.

Death and God
Faith in the resurrection means that we give thanks to God. To give thanks is to respond to a gift. If the fitting response

to Jesus' resurrection is to give thanks, then it is in this way that the believer will express his conviction that it is for him and *to his benefit* that God has identified himself with the dead Jesus. This is clearly what Paul means when he writes: 'For it is all for your sake' (2 Cor. 4: 15), and when he says: 'Thanks be to God who gives us the victory through our Lord Jesus Christ' (1 Cor. 15: 57). This is a statement which refers to a victory over death which will become an *indisputable* reality only 'when the last trumpet shall sound' (1 Cor. 15: 52). Nevertheless, it is this victory which the believer has already been granted by God. The victory over death is one which is already won.

It was won when God identified himself with the dead Jesus. As we have seen from our examination of the Old Testament, death means relationlessness. As the wages of sin, a view which we find more in the New Testament, death is the consequence of man's pernicious drive toward this relationlessness. Man's disastrous urge toward the deadliness of relationlessness stands in direct proportion to death's aggressiveness as alienating man from God and as breaking up human relationships. Now while in the Old Testament God is understood as standing at an infinite distance from death, wholly untouched by the deadliness of relationlessness, in the death of Jesus he endures contact with death. By identifying himself with the dead Jesus, God truly exposed himself to the alienating power of death. He exposed his own divinity to the power of negation. And he did precisely this in order to be God *for all men*.

To be for someone means to stand in a relationship with him. However, when God's relationship to us remains unbroken even in death, when he identifies himself with the dead Jesus in order to demonstrate his gracious concern for all men through the crucified One, then out of the midst of the relationlessness of death there emerges a *new relationship* between God and man. And we must be careful to note that this new relationship of God to man consists in God himself bearing the relationlessness of death which alienates man from him. It is when relationships are broken, when the relationships between men are ruptured that God takes up man's cause. As pledging himself for man in this way, God *reveals* his very being. By identifying himself with the dead Jesus of Nazareth to the benefit of all men, he reveals himself to finite man as a being of infinite *love*. For it is when everything has become relationless that love alone creates new relationships. When all relationships have been broken, only love can create new ones.

Love therefore is not only the motive behind God's actions, it is the very essence of his being. It is God's love which determines his action and all that he is in himself. It is because of love that God is moved to give new life to the dead, to that which is negative and accursed. He does this in such a way that he does not shrink from death, negation or the curse. In order to bring life and death into a new relationship with one another, into a new relationship which merits the name 'resurrection from the dead', God, through love, shares the pain of death. The statement of the ancient church with regard to *the incarnation* is not one which should be repeated without at the same time making this declaration. God's becoming man implies that God shares with man the misery of death. If the statement did not carry this implication then it would amount to little more than a verbal flourish. Nevertheless, properly understood, it is this statement which is definitive for the Christian understanding of the word 'God'. Aristotle was firmly opposed to the idea that God's being could be moved by others in his love toward them, nor, he argued, could God in any way be moved by the suffering of others. In the Old Testament it is assumed that God can have no concern for the dead (to say nothing of identifying himself with a dead man). However, according to the Christian understanding it is precisely what these positions seek to deny that Christian faith is bound to affirm. And these are the affirmations which must be made if we are really and truly to speak of *God*.

This is why we cannot adequately speak of the resurrection of Jesus without at the same time proclaiming his death as the *event of salvation*. The new relationship between God and man which emerges out of the relationlessness of death is the creation of a *new man*. However, this new man is not created out of an original nothing. He is created anew out of the nothingness and annihilation which are the consequences of his guilt and of his tendency toward self-destruction, the consequences which follow when he loses and forfeits his life. The creation of a new man cannot in any sense mean that he should spring 'slender and free as out of nothing'. The creation of a new man involves nothing less than the overcoming of that nothingness and annihilation which are the consequences of man's tendency toward self-destruction and of his guilt.

In any attempt to do justice to the resurrection we must speak of the overcoming of the curse of death and of the event of the divine love. Only in this way shall we be able to understand it as a life and death struggle. In God's *endurance* of death, the being of God and the being of death encounter one another. It is in and through this encounter that our own being is put in question.

In terms of the Easter-faith, this encounter is understood as a struggle. It is a struggle which begins with Jesus' life and which will be decided by his death. This encounter had its beginnings when Jesus brought the presence of God to the poor, the wretched, the social outcasts—including the wealthy sinners! when he healed the sick and cast out demons. For to be driven toward relationless and so drawn into the whirlpool of death is something which finds its expression in poverty and wretchedness, in social ostracism and isolation, in disease and in the demonic. Already in Jesus' life on earth we see God on the way toward death.

The Easter stories describe the outcome of this encounter. They tell of a *victory*. However, it is significant that the description is not of a God who strides through the gates of death as though through a triumphal arch. Death is not vanquished by simply disposing of it and leaving it behind. The pagan myths of the gods which describe how the gods die and return only to die again in the course of the cycle of the

years show that even if death is left behind it will only return
again to confront one anew. Death remains. All that happens is
the eternal recurrence of the same. By contrast, however, the
One who has been raised from the dead remains the crucified
One. And the marks of his dominion which he will forever bear
are the scars on his body.

This means then that God's victory over death which
Christians proclaim and in which they believe consists in his
bearing the contradiction of death in himself. Certain animals
die when they have emitted all their poison. Death as the
consequence of sin is like this kind of animal. Faith's
triumphant question: 'Death where is thy sting?' (1 Cor. 15: 55)
has only one answer. Death left, and had to leave its 'sting',
the instrument of its power, in the life of God.

And to this question of the prophet Hosea (13: 14), posed
in the certainty of victory, Paul immediately adds: 'The sting
of death is sin, and the power of sin is the law' (v. 56). The
intention of this additional remark is to demonstrate the extent
to which death has lost its annihilating power. For according
to Paul, God's identification with the dead Jesus means that
it was *on our behalf* that God made him who was free from sin
to be sin for us: 'For our sake he made him to be sin who knew
no sin' (2 Cor. 5: 21). In the terminology current in the
ancient world with regard to the ransom of slaves and
prisoners: 'Christ redeemed us from the curse of the law, having
become a curse for us—for it is written, "Cursed be every one
who hangs on a tree"' (Gal. 3: 13). Sin is aggression against
God. This is why it leads to death. As the law demanded, this
was the 'sting' which gave death its power. In *suffering* this
sting and by *enduring* the negation directed against him, God
robbed death of its power and so revealed himself as God. This
God loves man and it is for this reason that he suffers for
man. Man's suffering is finite. God, however, is not the kind
of God who does not suffer at all. He is the God who has a
capacity for *infinite* suffering, and it is because of his love that
he suffers infinitely. *This* is why he is death's conqueror.

This is why the reign of death is subject to the power of God.

With these last considerations we have penetrated to the very centre of Christian faith. This is something which can be expressed in various ways. However, no description of the essence of Christian faith—or better—no attempt to speak *from* the essence of Christian faith may omit this fact: Christ's death concerns us only because it is of concern to God. Every attempt, whether theological, dogmatic or liturgical, to hold God aloof and apart from the wretchedness of this death, fails to penetrate to the central core of Christian faith.

There is one traditional view of the death of Jesus Christ which must be expressly rejected as a misunderstanding. Based upon certain formulations to be found in the New Testament it is the view that the death of Jesus is to be understood as a human sacrifice to the God of wrath, as an offering intended to appease the wrathful God, who 'like the raging sea seeks out his victim'. No! If we are to speak of any offering at all in connection with the death of Jesus then it must be of the offering of divine otherness, of the surrender of the divine impassibility and absoluteness; in brief, of the sacrifice and surrender of the sheer distinctiveness of God over against his sinful creature. This is what is involved when we speak of God's identification with the dead Jesus. It was not that God let *himself* be reconciled through the death of Jesus. Enmeshed in its alienation from him, it was he who reconciled the *world* to himself (2 Cor. 5: 18f.). God is the one who reconciles and it is the world that is reconciled. It is man who is to be addressed concerning the reconciliation which he has effected (2 Cor. 5: 20).

To speak to man of the reconciliation which God has brought about means that his eyes should be opened to the fact that man's godlessness and guilt leave their marks upon God himself. In his concerned involvement with the sinner who must suffer the curse of death, God is also involved with man in his godlessness and guilt. It is by taking this godlessness and guilt upon himself that he opposes and contradicts them. Whenever we speak of God's identification with the dead Jesus this is what we mean. Luther expressed this as follows: on the cross, Christ is now 'the greatest robber of all, the greatest murderer, adulterer and thief; the greatest desecrator of temples and blasphemer; the world has seen none greater than this.'[6] However, it is only when the believer can *rejoice* in his need to perceive the marks which his own godlessness has left upon God himself that this statement will be seen to express the very essence of Christian faith. The marks which man's godlessness has left upon God himself are the visible signs of *reconciliation*. In terms of the language of the doctrine of justification, this would be the most concise way of expressing the meaning of the death of Jesus Christ.

Chapter Six

The Death of Death
(Death as this Present Life made Eternal)

The two dimensions of the biblical understanding of death
The biblical understanding of death is two-dimensional. It includes, *on the one hand*, a *statement* about the *essential nature* of death: death is the event of relationlessness in which the relationships in which man's life is lived are completely broken off. As the event of relationlessness it marks the end of a life-history, the end of a history of a soul with its body, the end of the whole person. As such it is therefore expressive of the finitude of human existence. When a man dies, he can only be what he was. To the extent that he has ceased to become anything, he has also ceased to be. For every present must presuppose a future. Without a future it would not be a present. The dead person 'is' only in the form in which he once existed. And it is in this form that the dead exist in relation to the history of the world. As giving some indication of what it is that death involves, it at least has the advantage of offering the natural sciences as well as the historical disciplines a basis for dealing with this problem. Both in the realm of nature and in the social or historical-political sphere it is the tendency toward relationlessness which makes for death. Moreover, with this definition of death there is also the possibility that 'nature' and 'history' may be conceived as a unity.

So much for the statement which defines one aspect of the essential nature of death. The *other* dimension of the biblical understanding of death presents itself as an *invitation* or *offer*. We are offered the message concerning the God who in participating in man's death *gains victory over death*. It is in connection with this invitation and the response to it that the difference between faith and unfaith is decided. Faith accepts the invitation. In doing so it projects itself as *hope* and at the same time undertakes an *obligation*.

Hope and obligation are grounded in the death of Jesus Christ. When threatened by death, the believer will not forget the One who has conquered death. From the very beginning man's life is threatened by death simply because his life issues in death. 'In the midst of life death surrounds us'. Yet for Luther this statement must be reversed as far as the Christian is concerned: 'in the midst of death we are surrounded by life.'[1] This is not meant to discredit the notion that man's life on earth is a continual dying. Nevertheless, the striking thing about Luther's suggestion is that a Christian can say and believe: whenever I am threatened by death, life has the victory. The Christian now has the right and the duty to *confront death with a threat*.

The *Ackermann aus Böhmen* describes a dispute with death.[2] Here the idea of meeting death with a threat is presented in a most impressive way. In terms which were quite unprecedented for the Middle Ages, the writer dares to question death's right to be one of God's officials.

The Easter-faith goes even further and speaks of death as an object of *scorn and derision*. This is not intended as a piece of metaphysical frivolity. However, if we are not to regard it as such then we must be clear about the extent to which one can threaten and deride death in a world so much in conflict and so visibly dominated by death in all its unbearably violent forms. To threaten and scorn death—what does this mean?

It is legitimised by the death of Jesus Christ. Through this event death is deprived of its power in the name of God. 'It was through his death,' as Luther liked to put it, 'that death itself was put to death.' The death of Christ is understood as *'the death of death.'* The metaphor is an effective one, and Luther can go on to intensify its harshness with the help of further apparently mythological expressions. There is the well-known Easter hymn: 'Scripture has proclaimed how one death devoured the other. Death has become the laughing-stock.'[3] As long as it cannot be expressed in any better way this harsh way of speaking must be allowed to stand. Indeed it would be difficult to find a better way of putting it.

However, we still have to see what significance the 'death of death' has for the *life* of the Christian. We shall attempt to answer this in what follows. In order to do so we shall offer an evaluation of the christological discussion of death and its relevance and importance for the general question of death. First of all we shall discuss the meaning and importance of the end of life, the end which still stands ineluctably before us despite the 'death of death'. It is here that faith's hope comes to expression as 'resurrection of the dead'. Only within this framework shall we be able to find an answer to the question concerning what it means to scorn and threaten death.

Death and time—the hope of faith

Man's existence is characterised by *temporality*. This is an anthropological insight into man's nature as a creature of God. The time which a man has will last as long as he lives. That which constitutes man's humanity is the fact that he has time. Man's essential being does not so much consist in the fact that he exists 'in time', but rather in the fact that the time he has as existing is simultaneously his lifetime. Man is a *temporal* being.

As existing temporally man has a present. However, the present never exists in and by itself. The present is always the result of what has gone before, of the past events which to a large extent have been decisive for the shape which the present must take. Every present is derived from the past. And in every present there is already always the intimation of a new present which we call the future. To this extent then, to exist temporally means to have a past and a future. A present without past and future would be an unhistorical abstraction, a moment of timelessness, an 'eternal now' (nunc stans), a moment of eternity, and therefore a self-contradiction.

In the stricter sense, temporal existence implies that man has a *history;* not merely a past history which is now behind him, but a future history which stands before him. However, it is in the present that man holds the threads of his history together, sorting out his past and projecting his future. In doing so man *communicates* with the others who in this same period of time have their own life-span, their own past and their own future. Were it not for the fact that man communicates he would have no history; that is to say, no time. It is only on the basis of historical communication that man can be said to have a history of his own, for it is only on the basis of community that man can possibly exist as an individual. However, it is because man should have his own history that he is granted time. Time is not an end in itself; it is the servant of man in the sense that it enables him to fulfil his history. Expressed in more conceptual terms this means that time is the formal ontological structure of the historicity of human existence.

Now how is this to be understood in theological terms? A man's life-time is fulfilled and becomes genuinely historical only when it is understood as a moment in God's history with all men. It was for the sake of this history that the world was created and it is in this sense that all men participate in this history. As a moment in this history each human lifetime has its own unique importance. It cannot be replaced by anything else. Man is replaceable in some of the roles which he accepts. However, even if he has spent it in empty talk, the life he has lived is irreplaceable. He was none other than himself.

However, the importance of this fact of the uniqueness of each man's life should not be misunderstood. We should not imagine that because of this our life is of infinite importance or that for the same reason our life can never end. The fact that it is a moment of God's history with all men makes it of unique importance to the infinite God. But that our life is regarded as uniquely important by the infinite God gives *us* no reason to conclude that *our* life is of infinite importance or indeed that human life can never end.

It is rather the case that as a *moment* in God's history with all men our life is *finite;* it has a beginning and an end. Of course prior to its beginning and beyond its end, temporal existence is in fact related to history. To the extent that its beginning and end constitute its limits, man's life, prior to its beginning, has a past. When it ends, it will have a future. That past, of course, is one in which that life had no part. Nevertheless, it was a past which was of considerable importance in shaping the destiny of that life. Similarly, that life has a future in which as such it will play no part, although again, it will have been effective in determining that future. It is through its earthly past and its this-worldly future lying beyond it that each human life receives its individual, historical value. It is within these boundaries that man has his own possibilities. To have been able to realise some of these possibilities will mean that he has lived his life.

However, this life is lived in relation to the history of God. This means therefore that this this-worldly life has an *eternal* past and an *eternal* future. As God's creation, life enters and is received into the resurrection of the dead.

However, the Christian resurrection hope should not be allowed to obscure the fact that this human life of ours is temporally limited. Although it frequently has been and will be interpreted in this way, the hope of resurrection cannot involve the expectation that life's temporal limitations will be dissolved. What would count against such a suggestion is the general anthropological observation that any dissolution of the temporal boundaries of human life would involve the dissolution of human individuality. To take an absurd example: a person who existed before his birth would be someone else. The same would hold with regard to the utopian postulate of a continuation of human life beyond death. In this connection 'I' would certainly be infinite. However, 'I' would not be I. On these general grounds alone, the hope of resurrection must be something quite different from hope in endless continuity.

However, we should also be rightly suspicious of all those views of 'eternal life' which conceive of it as a kind of heavenly compensation for earthly renunciation and as in this sense involving the dissolution of the temporal limitations of human life. 'I also was born in Arcadia/, but the prime of life brought only tears/ . . . / I have sacrificed all my joys to you/, Now I cast myself before your judgement throne./ . . . / From you, the rewarder, I demand requital.' Often enough this has also been the attitude of Christian piety. However, the ending of the poem calls for reflection and should not be regarded as quite so unchristian: 'All eternity cannot bring back/that which you omit in the moment.'

At any rate, the decisive thing is that the Christian hope of resurrection is *not* an *egoistic* conception. According to Paul the real objective of the resurrection of the dead is 'that God may be everything to every one' (1 Cor. 15: 28). Hope in *God* is essentially resurrection hope. This hope is also hope in salvation only to the extent that it is directed toward a God who saves. Salvation then, can only mean that it is *the life man has lived* that is saved, not the man is saved *out* of this life. The meaning of salvation is that God saves this life which we live. It involves the participation of this earthly, limited life in the life of God; the sharing of this temporally limited life in God's eternity; the participation of a life which has incurred guilt in the glory of God. To share in God's glory means that man is honourably acquitted of his guilt. It is as finite that man's finite life is *made eternal*. Not by endless extension—there is no immortality of the soul—but through participation in the very life of God. Our life is *hidden* in his life. In this sense the briefest form of the hope of resurrection is the statement: 'God is my eternity'. He will make everything whole; everything, including what we have been. Our *person* will then be our *manifest history*.

This understanding of resurrection is based upon the preceding exposition of the significance of the death and resurrection of Jesus Christ. We have seen in this connection that the decisive thing was the Pauline axiom that the risen One is proclaimed as the crucified One. It is not just a matter of saying that this dead man is alive or that he lives on. The resurrection does not cancel out the crucifixion. One further important point was that it is the risen One who *reveals* the *truth* of death and also the truth of Jesus' life in its involvement with death.

Accordingly, we must now consider the question of the resurrection of *all* men. Resurrection concerns the life man has actually lived. It is this life which will be delivered and honoured. Then, unlike the deceased who are separated from the bereaved, we shall be with God. It is as we have been that we shall all be gathered to God. Then we shall be *in* God who himself is *life*. We are not to imagine a collection of antiquities in a museum. The past which is redeemed is no mere past. The past which is redeemed is a past in the presence of God. It is he who makes it present to himself, and in so doing—here at least the word is appropriate—glorifies it. The past in the presence of God cannot in any sense be a dead past. It is rather a history made *articulate*, a history brought to expression before God and by God. Then, along with those aspects of our lives which have remained hidden to ourselves and to others, we ourselves shall stand revealed. The person who in his earthly life once claimed to have really known himself will then have cause to be ashamed of himself. (It is understood that for this purpose a special corner will be prepared for philosophers—bad ones!). Then we shall know even as we are now known by God (1 Cor. 13: 12). What we are now is what God now knows us to be. This is how we shall have been, and it is as we have been that we shall inherit eternity. Resurrection of the dead means then that it is the life we have actually lived that is gathered into community, made eternal and made manifest.

What we have been saying so far may be summarised in the words of one of the church's teachers: 'Man *as such* therefore, has no beyond. Nor does he need one, for God is his beyond. Man's beyond is that God as his Creator, Covenant-partner, Judge and Saviour, was and is and will be his true Counterpart in life, and finally and exclusively and totally in death. Man as such, however, belongs to this world. He is thus finite and mortal. One day he will only have been, as once he was not. His divinely given promise and hope and confidence in this confrontation with God is that even as this one who has been he will share the eternal life of God himself. Its content is not, therefore, his liberation from his this-sidedness, from his end and dying, but *positively* the glorification by the eternal God of his natural and lawful this-sided, finite and mortal being. He does not look and move towards the fact that this being of his in his time will one day be forgotten and extinguished and left behind, and in some degree replaced by a new, other-sided, infinite and immortal being after his time. More *positively*, he looks and moves towards the fact that *this being of his in his time*, and therewith its beginning and end before the eyes of the gracious God, and therefore before his own eyes and those of others, will be revealed in all its merited shame but also its unmerited glory, and may thus be eternal life from and in God. He does not hope for redemption from the this-sidedness, finitude and mortality of his existence. He hopes *positively* for the revelation of its redemption as completed in Jesus Christ, namely, the redemption of his this-sided, finite and mortal existence' (Barth).[4]

Death and equality—a socio-political consideration

Hope of resurrection arises within the context of our *obligation* to '*scorn death.*' Properly understood, however, hope of resurrection gives rise to yet another factor which must in this regard be taken into account. It concerns the relationship between death and the equality of all men.

That *all* men must die is something which man has had to learn. An aspect closely related to this, namely, that death involves the *resolution of all the distinctions* which determine man's

life, was regarded as even less self-evident. That death makes
all men equal was also something which men had to learn for
themselves. For a long time, and to a large extent even today,
social differences are decisive not only for the way in which we
live our lives, but also for everything we do in our endeavour
to come to terms with death.

This clearly derives first of all from the fact that death, as
the end of a man's life, involves the departure of one who has
occupied a particular role in society, a role which within a
human society is to a greater or lesser extent relevant and
important, and which accordingly has its effect upon that
society. The disturbance within a group due to the death of the
person who during his life dominated that group, is, even today,
quite different from the consternation which may be caused, for
example, by the death of a new-born child, or of someone who
has had a less significant role to play in society. The value of
a man's function in the life of a society tends not to be
measured in terms of his life as an individual. It is precisely in
the event of death that its value and significance for the
community is fully realised. This is understandable, and within
certain limits not only inevitable but even essential. Death
involves the departure of a man who has lived a particular life
and who to that extent has also played a quite specific role in
society. Accordingly, the consequences of having relinquished
his social role due to death will differ in each particular case.
Beyond the moment of departure the deceased not only becomes
part of the collective memory. With its postulate of the
continued survival of the dead, the collective imagination sees
them as destined for certain specific and different roles. It was
not always realised that death is the equaliser. Types of death
(suicide!), and even different forms of burial (cremation!) could
be employed as principles for differentiating one kind of 'life
after death' from another.

The Christian faith has strongly opposed these notions of
death. With its unambiguously strict idea of the equality of all
men before God in their relationship to him, it understands

death as the event which brings to an end all the distinctive roles which have shaped man's life. The late-mediaeval presentations of the dance of death lay powerful emphasis on death as the great equaliser.[5] In the Basel Death-Dance, for example, death summons the *emperor* to dance to 'the sound of his pipe' and the emperor replies: 'I could easily increase my empire/through battle and strife, and by checking wrong:/ Now death has so prevailed over me,/that I am an emperor no more.'

The *cripple*, whom death also names as serving no useful function in the world, greets death as a friend: 'A poor cripple here on earth/is of no value to any friend:/but death will be his friend/and accept him along with the rich.'

And the *Jew*, who in the Middle Ages was regarded as so very different from other men, is also made equal with other men by death: 'I want you now with me,/for to me you're just another man.'

Pope, emperor, cripple, Jew—death comes to *all men*. It makes all men equal. Nevertheless, to the extent that in the end this understanding of death renders all social distinctions relative, it also had certain repercussions upon the life of society. It has been rightly observed that the understanding of death portrayed in the dances of death present a lesson in social equality and demonstrate a tendency toward democracy. And the connections here between this conception of death and the social upheavals of the time should not be overlooked.

This discovery of death's egalitarianism is intimately bound up with faith in the justification of the sinner through the death of Jesus Christ in at least two respects.

The one New Testament principle with regard to death which Paul affirms in the context of his doctrine of justification ran: 'Death is the wages of sin' (Rom. 6:26). In death sin pays out the currency of death. As for sin, however, all men are involved in it; all men have sinned (Rom. 3:23). Death therefore holds sway over all men. In whatever sense it is to be under-stood, the Christian dogma of original sin carries with it a claim which applies to all men without distinction. In thus limiting man in a *negative* sense it is effective in reinforcing the idea of the equality of all men. The importance of this claim and its effect upon the history of western society is almost beyond assessment.

Related to this, but more important than this negative aspect is the other motivation toward 'democratisation' in the Christian understanding of death. This *positive* motivation finds expression in Paul's statement concerning the fact that man is justified by faith, by faith alone, as Luther appropriately translates it—and not by the works which the law demands of him (Rom. 3: 28). That God does not pronounce man just on the basis of human accomplishments quite obviously means that man is not justified by God on the basis of his social function, nor because of the role which he occupies in human society. To be justified by God and to stand justified before him is to receive justification for living, to be entitled to live our lives joyfully. No-one receives this justification or entitlement by reason of whatever it may be that gives a man importance within a society. No matter what he does or fails to do *every* man has the right and is entitled to live and to live joyfully, for regardless of men's works it was for all men that Jesus died.

The God who justifies is no respecter of persons. However, God does distinguish between the person and the work, role or function etc. This far-reaching distinction between what we are and what we and others make of our lives clearly demonstrates the fact that before God all men are equal. It was due to this that faith was first able to discover death's equalising role. Faith was able to do this without lapsing into cynicism, the kind of cynicism which is pleased to view the end which confronts all men as on the same level as that of an animal. This can also give rise to the suggestion that man, if in the end he is to suffer the same fate as an animal in any case, should be prepared to commit any crime in order to make his life more pleasurable (cf. Eccl. 3: 19f., and 9: 3f.). The

assertion that precisely the same end is reserved for both man
and beast prevents the discovery of any democratic 'motif' with
regard to man's death which could be made fruitful for society.
It arrives only at a final meaninglessness which makes every
human effort appear to be of no avail: in the end, the result
will be the same after all, irrespective of whether one has done
great things in life or nothing at all, irrespective of whether
one has lived as a man or as an animal. This is the kind of
cynicism which finds that it cannot cope with life's transitoriness.
It cannot cope because it cannot bear that things should pass
away.

However, the lesson in social equality which the Christian
understanding of death was able to impart had, as it were, to
face the threat of suspension. The reason for this was that it was
the person of the believer, as distinct from his works, that was
said to share in a life that was *eternal* and thus infinitely
superior to earthly life. The implications of this were that it
was only beyond death that persons could be regarded as equal.
Prior to death there could therefore be no equality. As long as
man's death was understood in the Platonic sense as the release
of the soul from the body, that is, purely as the death of the body
and therefore as in no way hindering the continued existence of
the human soul, it could be agreed that equality was
reserved for the life beyond death. In contrast to this, however,
when death is radically understood as the end of human life
then the lesson of social equality which this implies is bound
to have an effect upon this-worldly life and to have certain
socio-political repercussions. This means that social distinctions
cannot by any means command any final respect. 'Egalité' thus
becomes a postulate, but its realisation will involve much more
than the recognition that under the guillotine all heads are the
same.

Death and anxiety—the obligation of faith
If it belongs to man's life that it should end in death, if
resurrection from the dead means not life's infinite con-

tinuation but that the life we have lived is gathered to that of others and made eternal, then the reconciling power of the death of Jesus Christ must be of benefit to man's *life*, to the time which he is allotted between life's beginning and end. Luther's famous statement from the Shorter Catechism also leaves us in no doubt about this: Jesus Christ, 'not with gold or silver, but with his sacred and precious blood, his sinless suffering and death, has saved, redeemed and rescued me, lost and condemned, from all sin and death and from the power of the devil, that I should live under him in his kingdom and serve him in everlasting righteousness, sinlessness and bliss.' But what does 'being saved from death' mean?

To be saved from death means to be set free for a new relationship to God and for a new relationship to oneself. This involves that the threat which we ourselves imagine we must meet at the end of our lives has lost its power, that the curse of those actions which cause us to lose and forfeit our lives is broken. The death of Jesus Christ has set us free from the law which in life and in death leaves us exposed to the nothingness of our actions (Rom. 8: 2). Salvation from death means therefore that we are set free *both* to live *and* to die. The person who cannot live also cannot die. This is a circle, which in its negative way—as Luther expresses it—describes the condition of the man who is 'lost and condemned': he can neither live nor die. And to be able neither to live nor to die is hell. And its power is destroyed through the death of Jesus Christ. To be able both to live and to die is the gift which Christ makes to his own: for 'if we live, we live to the Lord, and if we die, we die to the Lord; so then, whether we live or whether we die, we are the Lord's' (Rom. 14: 8).

This circle in which we are involved with the notion of being both able to live and to die has also a positive aspect. The be able to die means to be able to live and *vice versa*. It was a fateful day when Christianity was misunderstood as being solely and finally concerned only with being able to die. It is offensive that one should be required to understand one's

entire life as a training for death. It was also due to pagan
influences that Christianity developed a form of 'ars moriendi',
an 'art of dying'. But the believer is not an artist in death.
And the reason for this is that as far as such an art is
concerned the tendency is for one's own 'I' to become
intolerably inflated. 'Ars moriendi' is, as it were, the most
refined way of distinguishing oneself from oneself in order to
make oneself interesting. No: it is impossible to be able to die
without being able to live.

To be able to die thus implies that one can say 'Yes' to
life. To affirm life also calls for the courage not to close one's
eyes to the necessity of death. The wish to keep life intact and
pure from every contact with death is an illusion. A life which
shrinks from death and which cannot bear the fact that it will
end, which endeavours at all costs to remain pure and intact, is
just as much an abstraction as one which longs for death and
which is concerned only with its own passing away and ending.
An abstract life is in itself untrue. For the living actualisation
of genuine life, the confrontation with death is essential.

We may illustrate this with reference to the phenomenon
of anxiety about death. Almost everyone is anxious about
death. But we should not confuse anxiety about death with
cowardice. This would be to misunderstand the real nature of
anxiety altogether. Anxiety is something quite different from
cowardice. Anxiety is something which life is able to use for its
own protection. To be anxious about something is one of the
essential features of man's humanity. Anxiety enables a man to
protect himself. In one's anxiety one is troubled about the
future outcome of one's present situation. This anxiety is most
intimately related to man's understanding of himself as the
creature who hopes. And it has been rightly observed that to
have no anxiety and no hope is to be inhuman (Jens).[6]

This clearly applies only with regard to the kind of anxiety
which is self-created. Anxiety artificially created is inhuman, or
more exactly, the artificial creation of anxiety is inhuman.
Anxiety here is perverted and becomes an instrument of

submission. The anxiety which is artificially induced is something which must be resisted, and one can achieve this best by resisting the one who is responsible for creating it.

However, the kind of anxiety which is self-creating and which is effective in protecting human life is not something which can be resisted. In order to overcome it one must recognise it and even to some extent give in to it. This is the case with regard to anxiety about death. It is human, profoundly human. It is in and through this anxiety that man's right to life finds its most fundamental expression. That the passion story makes no exception of Jesus when it comes to the question of being anxious about death is something which ought to remind us that faith does not exempt the Christian from being anxious about it. Faith as little excludes anxiety about death as it artificially creates anxiety about death. Nevertheless, faith is able to recognise it as a fact.

The aim therefore cannot be to allay anxiety about death. This would only lead to replacing a healthy anxiety about death with a more or less neurotic anxiety about one's anxiety about death. And the result of this would be to suppress the fact of the necessity of death.

It is therefore more fitting that we should meet anxiety about death with *concern for life*. Anxiety about death is anxiety about relationlessness. Concern for life expresses itself as concern for the relationships within which men may honourably live their lives. It is because of its care for man's relationship to God that faith is able to meet and deal with anxiety about death. Yet it is impossible to be concerned about the relationship between God and man without at the same time being concerned for the relationships between man and man. When the last hour has struck, when a person's hope can be directed only toward the One who alone can receive that life now completed to himself, at this point also, the relationships of the person to those from whom he is to be separated form part of his relationship to God. One can die at peace only when one could have continued to live at peace with others.

Meeting and dealing with anxiety about death also means being actively concerned for the person who has this anxiety. If anxiety about death functions as protecting human life, then it becomes necessary to examine what sort of *threat* it is which this anxiety seeks to resist. In this respect, the nature of the threat is twofold. On the one hand, we have to face up to all those different kinds of threats which conspire to bring our life to an untimely end. But, on the other hand, there is another kind of threat. We might call it the threat which the human self poses to itself.

The threat which the self poses to itself is actualised in those active and passive moments in human conduct which are determined by what we have termed the impulse toward relationlessness, or, in other words, by sin. That which causes the self to pose a threat to itself can be seen in its tendency to ascribe absolute value to itself, in its tendency to assume that it is the final criterion of all values. This can happen, for example, when the self regards its life as its own private possession. In biblical terms this is to say that it is when the 'I' is solely concerned with finding itself that it poses a threat to itself. The person who in everything seeks his own self will lose himself. The person who is always in pursuit of his own identity runs the risk of neither finding himself nor anything else for that matter. The person who is not free from himself is unable to become genuinely involved in reality with its events in time and its historical occurrences, to say nothing whatever of becoming involved with other people. In the endeavour to realise himself, man loses those possibilities which make human existence human. He remains concerned only with himself.

A life so concerned only with itself must inevitably fail to grasp the essential purpose and function of the time which is allotted to it. As we have seen, time is the form of God's history with us. Our lifetime, accordingly, is not an end in itself but a sphere of historical encounter. A life solely concerned with itself and thus concretely demonstrating its impulse toward relationlessness in this way is quite unable to lay hold of time as the sphere of historical encounter. The time which is given to a life can thus be seen in only one of its aspects: it expires. Time runs out. And the consequence of this is that when the time allotted to this life has finally expired, the self-concerned self finds itself confronted with nothingness. This is what gives rise to dread— and rightly so. Death reveals the nothingness of such a life. And it is this which causes the anxiety to become more intense. This intensification of anxiety concerning death is the way in which the self of itself is able to react to the threat which it poses to itself.

Such intense anxiety about death is a symptom, an alarm signal. It is set in motion of itself. It would be irresponsible for someone to want to create such anxiety. Christian preachers and pastors cannot be absolved from having committed a great many serious mistakes in this respect. Anxiety about death which is artifically created is something entirely different from the kind of anxiety which life itself makes use of as a self-protective reaction. It is a crime against life. To create anxiety about death only in order to be able to witness to Jesus Christ as Saviour from death is to do thoroughly objectionable theological business with death. When it comes to proclaiming Jesus Christ this kind of folly is quite uncalled for. However, what the proclamation does enable us to do is to address and analyse anxiety about death wherever it actually occurs. And it also enables us to lift the threat with which life threatens itself and which is concealed in this anxiety.

For the elimination of this threat with which life threatens itself (a tendency which lies dormant in all men), the remedy which is offered is *reconciliation*. The man who is reconciled to God does not need to seek himself in everything. The one who continually set out to find himself is now found. Not of course by himself, but by God. This means that he now need have no fear of losing himself in death. He will not go astray. Of course he awaits his own end in death. However, his hope is that it will be God himself who will limit and surround him in death. It makes all the difference whether it is nothingness that sets that limit to man in death or God. But the difference is all the greater whether nothingness sets the limit to man in his death or a *gracious* God. It is the hope that it is a gracious God who limits and surrounds his life that gives man the courage to scorn death, hell and the devil. These terms, hell and devil, give expression to the triumph of that relationlessness which threatens the sinner in death. But even this threat holds no terror for the believer. The believer sets his hope against the threat that in the end his life will prove to be meaningless. And his hope is directed not toward his life, with the dignity of its good works and the burden of its misdeeds. It is directed toward God alone. Armed with this hope in life, death is deprived of its power. And we might call this a *spiritual scorning of death.* Just as Luther scorned the devil: 'And so the devil will be fooled, finding himself threshing empty straw. For what are you fighting, devil? Are you trying to find good works, to find fault with my own holiness before God? Serves you right, for I have neither! The power which I have is not my own; the *Lord* is my strength . . . I have no knowledge of either sin or holiness in me. I know nothing, nothing but God's power in me.'[7]

A quite different threat to which life reacts by being anxious about death is the *threat of an untimely or unnatural death.* We have seen that freed from the curse of death by the death of Jesus Christ, human life has a natural end which comes when the time allotted to a life has expired. Man has the right to die this death and no other. One of the duties of Christian faith is to see that this right is recognised. There is therefore an immediate connection between the proclamation of the death of Jesus Christ and the *concern that man should have the right to die a natural death.*

This means that there is definite work to be done to improve those conditions prevailing in the world which shape and regulate our lives. The right to a natural death is something which has to be earned—in political, medical and social terms. To this extent we find ourselves in agreement with Werner Fuchs. Taking the notion of natural death as his basic concept, Fuchs argues against any notion of death as being to supernatural causes. He also uses it to make certain polemical points in connection with the question of violent death due to unnatural causes. Along with this concept of natural death goes the assumption that medical science has the capacity to limit death to the death which comes as a result of the weakness of old age. It is also based on the presupposition that certain policies should be developed for the attainment of similar ends. To this extent then, the concept 'is charged with social-critical power. It calls for a social constitution in which natural death is taken to be the rule, or where there is at least the possibility of it becoming the rule.'[8] The notion of natural death in this sense 'thus gives rise to the principle that in order to make natural death at all possible, the conditions for it must first be created.'

To make natural death possible for all men means to scorn and threaten death *in the world*. To mock at death is certainly not to scorn life. To threaten death is to refrain from posing any threat to life. Since faith knows God and God alone as the boundary of man's life, it is involved in social terms in a struggle against death. Hope in the God who in death shelters and surrounds us sets us free from egoistic concern about our own end. That which takes its place is a concern for the life of others. To every person a time is allotted so that in their own time they may also have their history. It is a matter for God and God alone to set life's temporal limits. It is faith's duty to protest openly against every attempt to claim the right to set temporal limits to human life. No man, no institution, no legal administration has the right to mark out the temporal boundaries of man's finite life. The Christian has the *duty* to oppose actively every effort to gain control of death. In every sphere of life, to have death at one's disposal is something thoroughly reprehensible. And if God has taken death upon himself in order to bind it to himself for ever, then death cannot any longer be regarded as a legal remedy. In the light of this, 'capital punishment' becomes a 'crimen laesae maiestatis', a 'lèse-majesté' against the crucified God.

Much the same applies with regard to the question of political calculation with death. Every war involves political calculation with the death of other men. By various methods the soldier's inhibitions about killing can be switched off and on. If, on his own responsibility, he goes on killing, (for once his inhibitions about killing have been suppressed they cannot so easily be re-created), the world rises up in indignation. But this indignant revolt comes too late. It should initially have been directed against the sheer absurdity of the fact that history, that for which we are given time, has been used to bring the lives of a great many people to an unnatural end. In scorning death we adopt precisely the opposite attitude of the strategy of killing whose alleged aim is the attainment of higher historical goals. To mock death— it is this attitude which must be made effective in the interest of *life and its right to a natural end.*

Clearly, a strategy of this kind will not only apply to those concrete dangers which accompany ageing and dying. It must rather oppose the *deadly tendency* toward relationlessness wherever and however it becomes apparent. This will call for far greater social-political activity and effort in the sphere of medicine and psychological medicine than ever before.

With the help of such a strategy, not only must the fact of life itself be guaranteed, it must also ensure that the *possibilities of life* can be allowed to develop. Life as mere existence is not life in the full meaning of the word. 'It is not life itself that is important; what is of sole importance is the development of life's possibilities' (Jores).[9] The view is somewhat exaggerated, but it is not entirely mistaken. It would amount to sheer sarcasm if one were to suggest that life should be preserved in such a way that every living creature in its time and with its possibilities should be allowed to atrophy. Old people in particular, who see themselves as left with only few possibilities, must be offered possibilities by others, so that in this late period of their lives they may still have joy until the time comes for them to die 'at a good age'.

To mock death therefore means to be concerned about life's possibilities and the development of these possibilities. This is also of importance for the shaping of conditions for life in a world *fraught with conflict*. The violent prevention of every conflict in the interest of a smoothly functioning society would deprive man of precisely that possibility of perceiving and laying hold of those possibilities which are given to him in an appropriate way. Because of the way in which man's life is socially determined, the present is at once both a sphere of communication and of conflict. Where contact and communication are concerned conflict is always involved. When communication is successfully effected, the conflict is fruitful. Even where it fails, the conflict need not always be frustrating. To bear and to endure such conflicts for the sake of the growth and development of human life is also one of man's ownmost possibilities. This is also the sphere of the conflict between faith and reason. In this respect, the faith which is based upon reconciliation with God passionately opposes every attempt to end conflict by violence. The complete absence of conflict spells death. The tendency toward it is the criterion of dictatorship and tyranny.

Not least, the possibility of enduring conflict can be of positive advantage for *the way in which we stand toward death*. Man's relationship with death is not free of conflict. In fact it is laden with conflict. All of these conflicts are always to be found within the context of life. Faith gives man the courage to bear them. It is only by bearing the conflicts of life which determine our relationship to death that anxiety about death can achieve its purpose of protecting life from an untimely end and from becoming eternally lost.

The essential nature of death is relationlessness. The deadly tendency toward relationlessness can always be checked by creating new relationships. These are the kind of relationships which will enable us to understand and accept the fact that man's finite life has its value precisely in its finitude—a finitude which can mock at death to the glory of God. In life, man can never resist death enough. Dying, he can do nothing at all against death. Death must be reduced to that limit which no man can set, for no man can abolish it. Death must be and must become what Jesus Christ has made it: the limit to man which is set by God alone, who, in our total powerlessness, never abuses his power. For when there is nothing we can do, he is there on our behalf. His purposes are wonderful and his power great.

Bibliography

CHAPTER ONE

1 For biblical passages see Gen. 25: 8; 1 Sam. 31: 4, 2; Matt. 27: 5; Gen. 5: 24.

2 Arthur Jores, *Der Tod des Menschen in psychologischer Sicht*, in *Der leidende Mensch*, Darmstadt, 1965.

3 Luke 2: 28ff.

4 Edward Young (1774), quotation taken from Josef Pieper's *Tod und Unsterblichkeit*, Munich, 1968, p. 29.

5 Sigmund Freud, cf. Pieper, op. cit., p. 83, and Freud's 'Thoughts on War and Death' in *The Complete Psychological Works of Sigmund Freud*, Vol. 14, London, 1957, p. 289.

6 Sophocles, *Antigone* (Lines 332–375); see also Martin Heidegger, *An Introduction to Metaphysics*, London, 1959, p. 158.

7 Max Scheler, 'Tod und Fortleben', from *Schriften aus dem Nachlass*, Vol. 1, Berne, 1957, p. 30.

8 Søren Kierkegaard, *The Concept of Irony*, London, 1966, pp. 286–287.

9 Augustine, *Enarrationes in Psalmos*, XXXVIII, 19.

10 Ludwig Wittgenstein, *Tractatus Logico-Philosophicus*, London, 1971, p. 147 (6.4311).

11 M. Scheler, op. cit., p. 22.

12 See J. Pieper, op. cit., p. 41, who correctly refers to this as a sophism. Epicurus' statement is to be found in his letter to Menoeceus.

13 M. Scheler, op. cit., p. 33 (Scheler's views on death as a legal question).

14 Paul Landsberg, *Die Erfahrung des Todes*, Lucerne, 1937, pp. 5f.

15 Jacques Choron, *Der Tod im abendländischen Denken*, Stuttgart, 1967, p. 13. This book is of considerable importance for our discussion as a whole.

16 Regarding 'proof' of mortality see, e.g., Ernst Cassirer, *The Philosophy of Symbolic Forms*, Vol. 2, New Haven/London, 1955, pp. 47–49.

17 M. Scheler, op. cit., pp. 16 and 20.

18 Augustine, *Confessions*, IV, 4.

19 Alcmaeon of Croton, see *The Presocratic Philosophers*, edited by G. S. Kirk and J. E. Raven, Cambridge, 1959, pp. 232–235.

[20] Rudolf Nissen, 'Leben und Tod: eine medizinisch-naturwissenschaftliche und ärztliche Betrachtung', in *Leben und Tod*, Basel o.J., p. 31.

[21] See the volume of collected essays, *Was ist der Tod?* Munich, 1969. Quotations given here from this volume are from essays by Hans Schaefer, 'Der natürliche Tod', see pp. 18 and 14, and Wilhelm Doerr, 'Vom Sterben', see pp. 62f.

[22] See Doerr, op. cit., p. 63; and Schaefer, op. cit., pp. 20f.

[23] Hans Kuhlendahl, *Zwischen Leben und Tod*, p. 89 and pp. 92f.

[24] See Adolf Faller, 'Biologisches vom Sterben und Tod', in *Anima*, 1956, pp. 260ff.

[25] Of importance in connection with this problem: Gerhard Ebeling, *Gott und Wort*, Tübingen, 1966; Eberhard Jüngel, 'Freiheitsrechte und Gerechtigkeit', in *Evangelische Theologie*, 1968, pp. 486–495, and *Die Freiheit der Theologie*, *Theologische Studien 88*, Zürich, 1967.

CHAPTER TWO

[1] Johann Gottlieb Fichte, *The Science of Rights*, London, 1889, p. 60.

[2] Paul Landsberg, op. cit., p. 30.

[3] Alois Hahn, *Einstellungen zum Tod und ihre soziale Bedingtheit, Eine soziologische Untersuchung*, Stuttgart, 1968. For passages cited in this section see pp. 16, 26 and 68.

[4] Bernhard Groethuysen, *Die Entdeckung der bürgerlichen Weltund Lebensanschauung in Frankreich*, Vol. 1, Halle, 1927, p. 95.

[5] A. Faller, op. cit., p. 260.

[6] Christian von Ferber, *Soziologische Aspekte des Todes*, in *Zeitschrift für Evangelische Ethik*, 1963, p. 341.

[7] Gustav Bally, *Das Todesproblem in der wissenschaftlich-technischen Gesellschaft*, in *Wege zum Menschen*, 1966, pp. 130 and 133.

[8] Karl Rahner, *The Experiment with Man* (*Theological Investigations*, Vol. 9), London, 1972, pp. 221–222.

[9] See e.g., Jessica Mitford, *The American Way of Death*, London, 1963.

[10] Werner Fuchs, *Todesbilder in der modernen Gesellschaft*, Frankfurt, 1969, p. 228.

[11] For the quotation from A. Comte see M. Scheler, op. cit., p. 15.

[12] This is the conclusion of an Emnid Poll, published by Werner Harenberg in *Was Glauben die Deutschen?* Munich/Mainz, 1968.

[13] M. Scheler, op. cit., p. 15.

[14] David Friedrich Strauss, *The Old Faith and the New: A Confession.* London, 1874.

[15] A. Hahn, op. cit., p. 110, note 8.

CHAPTER THREE

[1] Aristotle, *Protrepticus.* See *The Works of Aristotle translated into English,* Vol. 12, Oxford, 1952, p. 41; also Werner Jaeger, *Aristotle,* Oxford, 1934, p. 100.

[2] W. Jaeger, op. cit., p. 99.

[3] Paul Friedländer, *Platon,* Vol. 3, Berlin, 1960. Passages cited in this chapter from pp. 30 and 35. For an interpretation of the *Phaedo* see R. Guardini, *Der Tod des Sokrates,* Reinbek, 1956.

[4] Plato, *The Last Days of Socrates (Phaedo),* Penguin Classics, 1969, p. 108.

[5] Karl Rahner, *Zur Theologie des Todes (Quaestiones Disputatae* 2), Freiburg, 1958, p. 18.

[6] Plato, op. cit., p. 116.

[7] Plato, op. cit., p. 168.

[8] Plato, op. cit., p. 107.

[9] Plato, op. cit., p. 143.

[10] Plato, op. cit., p. 178.

[11] Cicero, *Tusculanae Disputationes,* I, 74.

[12] Aristotle, *Metaphysics,* A 982 b 12f.

[13] Gotthold Ephraim Lessing, *Wie die Alten den Tod gebildet, eine Untersuchung,* 1769.

[14] Homer, *The Odyssey,* Book 11. (See Penguin Classics edition, trans. E. V. Rieu, London, 1946, p. 189).

[15] Plato, op. cit., p. 138.

[16] Georg Friedrich Wilhelm Hegel, *Phenomenology of Mind,* trans. J. B. Baillie, London, 1910, Preface, pp. 29–31.

Of general interest for Chapter Three/p. 00 see: *Unsterblichkeit,* Norbert Luyten, Adolf Portmann, Karl Jaspers, Karl Barth, Basel, 1966; Oscar Cullmann, *Immortality of the Soul or Resurrection of the Dead?,* London, 1958.

[17] Walter Bernet, *Gebet (Themen der Theologie,* Vol. 6), Stuttgart, 1970, pp. 87f.

CHAPTER FOUR

1 Of general interest for this section see J. Pieper, op. cit., Part I/2. See also p. 14 for quotation from Schopenhauer, and Schopenhauer's *Werke*, Insel Verlag, Vol. 2, Leipzig, p. 1240.

2 Gerd Schunack, *Das hermeneutische Problem des Todes*, Tübingen, 1967, pp. 50ff.

3 Ludwig Köhler, *Hebrew Man*, London, 1956, p. 46.

4 L. Köhler, op. cit., p. 49.

5 Gottfried Quell, *Die Auffassung des Todes in Israel*, Darmstadt, 1967 (Leipzig, 1925), p. 6.

6 L. Köhler, op. cit., p. 112.

7 Martin Luther, *Vorlesung über I Mose 26: 24* (WA 43, 481, 32–35).

8 Martin Noth, *The Old Testament World*, London, 1966, p. 173. See also Ludwig Wächter, *Der Tod im Alten Testament*, Berlin, 1967.

9 G. Quell, op. cit., p. 22.

10 Victor Maag, 'Tod und Jenseits nach dem Alten Testament', in *Schweizerische Theologische Umschau*, 1964, pp. 17–37, especially pp. 22f.

11 L. Köhler, op. cit., p. 110.

12 L. Köhler, op. cit., pp. 112–113.

13 See Ulrich Wilckens, *Auferstehung* (*Themen der Theologie*, Vol. 4), Stuttgart, 1970.

14 See Ernst Fuchs, *Zur Frage nach dem historischen Jesus*, Tübingen, 1965, which is of importance for this section and for Chapter Five.

15 Karl Rahner, op. cit., (Part III/2) p. 45.

16 K. Rahner, op. cit., pp. 37f.

17 Ladislaus Boros, *Mysterium Mortis*, Olten, 1967, p. 42.

18 On the notion of the second death see L. Wächter, op. cit., p. 42; Wilhelm Brandt, *Das Schicksal der Seele nach dem Tode*, Darmstadt, 1967, (Jahrbücher für protestantische Theologie, 1892), p. 46.

19 Plato, op. cit., pp. 170–171.

20 Augustine, *City of God*, Book 13, 2, 11.

CHAPTER FIVE

Of importance for the entire chapter: *Das Kreuz Jesu Christi als Grund des Heils*, Schriftenreihe des Theologischen Ausschusses der EKU, edited by Fritz Viering, Gütersloh, 1967.

1 Martin Kähler, *The So-called Historical Jesus and the Historic Biblical Christ*, Philadelphia, 1964, p. 80, note 11.

2 Herbert Braun, *Jesus* (Themen der Theologie Vol. 1), Stuttgart, 1969, p. 167.

3 Plato, op. cit., pp. 100–101.

4 Thomas Aquinas, *Summa Theologica* III, 7, 3, c.

5 Gerhard Ebeling, *Was heisst: Ich glaube an Jesus Christus?* in *Was heisst: Ich glaube an Jesus Christus?* Zweites Reichenau-Gespräch der Evangelischen Landessynode Württemberg, Stuttgart, 1968, pp. 38–77.

6 Martin Luther, *Vorlesung über Gal. 3: 13* (WA 40/1, 433, 26 28).

CHAPTER SIX

1 Martin Luther, *Predigt am Tage Mariä Heimsuchung*, (WA 11, 141, 22; cf., 40/3, 496, 3f.).

2 On the *Ackermann aus Böhmen* see Walter Rehm, *Der Todesgedanke in der deutschen Dichtung*, Darmstadt, 1967 (Halle, 1927), pp. 115ff.

3 Martin Luther, *Nach Hosea 13: 14, Osterpredigt 1524*, (WA 15, 518, 26f.); also *Auslegung von Gal. 2: 19*, (WA 40/1, 267, 1), *Gal. 3: 13*, (WA 40/1, 440, 13).

4 Karl Barth, *Church Dogmatics*, III/2, Edinburgh, 1960, pp. 632–633.

5 On the 'lesson' of the dance of death see W. Fuchs, op. cit., pp. 59f. and bibliography.

6 Walter Jens, in *Angst und Hoffnung in unserer Zeit*, Darmstädter Gespräch, ed. Karl Schlechta, Darmstadt, 1965, p. 165. See also Thure von Uexküll, pp. 17f. Also of importance for this section: Klaus Schwarzwaller, *Die Angst—Gegebenheit und Aufgabe (Theologische Studien* 102), Zürich, 1970.

7 Martin Luther, *Confitemini, Ps. 118: 17*, (WA 31/1, 149, 13–150, 6).

8 W. Fuchs, op. cit., (Sect. II/2), p. 72.

9 Arthur Jores, 'Lebensangst und Todesangst', in *Die Angst*, Studien aus dem C. G. Jung-Institut, Zürich, 1959, p. 181.